William Eleroy Curtis

A Summer Scamper Along the old Santa Fe Trail

And Through the Gorges of Colorado to Zion

William Eleroy Curtis

A Summer Scamper Along the old Santa Fe Trail
And Through the Gorges of Colorado to Zion

ISBN/EAN: 9783744753869

Printed in Europe, USA, Canada, Australia, Japan

Cover: Foto ©Andreas Hilbeck / pixelio.de

More available books at **www.hansebooks.com**

A Summer Scamper

Along the Old
  Santa Fe Trail
    and Through the
      Gorges of Colorado
        to Zion.

BY

WILLIAM E. CURTIS.

CHICAGO:
THE INTER-OCEAN PUBLISHING COMPANY.
1883.

CONTENTS.

I. THE ROMANCE OF WESTERN HISTORY.
II. STORIES OF THE OLD SANTA FE TRAIL.
III. ARMY AND INDIAN LIFE ON THE BORDER.
IV. HEROES OF THE OLD SANTA FE TRAIL.
V. TO THE AZTEC NAZARETH.
VI. THE PEAKS AND CANONS OF COLORADO.
VII. THE CITY OF THE SAINTS.

A Summer Scamper.

CHAPTER I.

THE ROMANCE OF WESTERN HISTORY.

WE are in the habit of thinking and speaking of the section west of the Missouri River as a new country, yet it was explored before New England, and is as rich in legendry and romance as the castle-crowned banks of the Rhine. From the mouth of the Kaw River, along "The Old Santa Fe Trail," every mile has its history of peaceful commerce and bloody warfare; and when the land of the Pueblos is reached, the antiquarian will find ruins as venerable as England's most ancient abbey, and customs that are as old as Egypt.

It was only thirty years after the discovery of this continent by Columbus, and nearly a century before the pious Pilgrims bowed their grateful knees upon "that stern and rock-bound coast," that an old buccaneer from Spain was rambling over the plains of Kansas, searching for Florida. His name was Alvar

Nunez Cabaza de Vaca, and he had three comrades with him, castaways from a wreck on the Gulf of Mexico.

Pamphilo de Narvaez sailed from the West Indies in 1520, or thereabouts, with four hundred men, in four ships, for Florida, of which he had been made Governor by the King of Spain. He lost his reckoning, entered the Gulf of Mexico, and was driven ashore somewhere on the coast of Louisiana or Texas. The vessel commanded by Cabaza de Vaca was capsized and all hands lost except the captain and three of his crew, who reached land and spent the next eight or nine years searching for a place they never found. They wandered westward, along the Valley of the Arkansas River, until they reached the Indian pueblos of New Mexico, where they heard from the nut-brown natives rumors of the invasion of the land of the Montezumas by Cortez. Upon the receipt of this news they abandoned their trip to Florida, and went to Mexico instead.

In the year 1530, Nuno de Guzman, the Governor of New Spain, as Mexico was then called, learned from some of his courtiers of fascinating stories that had been told by an Indian slave, of seven cities lying to the northward, more splendid than were ever seen; whose streets were paved with silver, and whose houses were made of gold. The lust of the Spaniard had been sharpened by the actual discoveries of Cortez in Mexico and Pizarro in Peru, and he set out with an army of many thousand men to raid and sack these seven cities of Cibola, or the Land of the Buffalo, as they were called. But he encountered many difficulties, was unable to subsist so large an army, and was compelled to go back. When Cabaza reached Mexico, the stories of what he had seen and heard stimulated the Spaniards to new exertions, and after several short journeys of exploration by different men, who returned without success, an expedition was organized under the command of a gallant and enduring fellow named Francisco Vasquez de Coronado, who went with orders not to return until he was able to bring back something worth carrying. The march of Coronado was one of the grandest in the history of the world. He was away three years, and in his ardent and persistent search for the cities of gold and silver, went as far as the Missouri, near where Omaha now stands, and would no doubt have gone still farther eastward but for his inability to cross the river. He traversed the State of Kansas twice, following very nearly the present line of the Atchison, Topeka & Santa Fe Railroad, and called the country Quivira.

In 1804, President Jefferson sent Merriweather Lewis, the son of one of his old neighbors, and William Clarke, up the Missouri River to its source in the Rockies, across the Grand Continental Divide, from which the head waters of the Columbia were followed in canoes to the sea. Upon his return from this exploration, which was only second to that of Coronado, Lewis was rewarded by being made Governor of the Territory of Missouri, which then included all of the Northwest; and Clarke succeeded him in office in 1813.

In 1804, Lieut. Zebulon Pike, of the Army, who

had just returned from exploring the Mississippi River to the Falls of St. Anthony, which now furnish the power for the great Minneapolis mills, was sent across the Continent to the southwest, as Lewis and Clarke had been sent in the other direction. Pike followed the Santa Fe Trail along the Arkansas River to where it plunges through the Royal Gorge, from its source near Leadville, and was lost in the mountains. He discovered the mighty peak which bears his name, and explored a great part of the Southern ranges of the Rockies, suffering almost incredible hardships, losing more than half his men, and all the horses, instruments, note books and other baggage he took with him. After spending two years in the mountains, he finally worked his way out and reached the Rio Grande River, in New Mexico, sixty or seventy miles from Santa Fe. Here he was discovered by the Mexicans, and his presence reported to the Governor. His Excellency sent out an officer to invite Pike to the capital, and he was glad to go; reaching the city with fifteen of the twenty-nine men who started from Missouri with him, half starved, hatless, bootless, and wearing grotesque garments they had made of the skins of animals. Poor Pike thought this invitation was an act of hospitality, and with his weary men supposed that their sufferings were over, but the Spanish authorities threw them into prison, seized and destroyed the most valuable papers he had preserved to show the results of his explorations, and endeavored to make a great sensation by asserting that Pike and his hungry Falstaffian escort had come there with a design of capturing the territory. It so happened that shortly before Pike left Missouri, Aaron Burr made a visit to the frontier, searching for the empire that had arisen in his dreams; but he reported Kansas a desert, and diverted his plans to Louisiana. The Burr conspiracy occurred while Pike was absent, and in the feverish state of public uneasiness there were many who had imaginations sufficiently vivid to see in the gallant explorer an emissary of Burr, marching through the Southwest at the head of a triumphant army, and conquering the country over which he was to rule. There could scarcely have been a wilder theory, but it was believed by many people, and poor Pike had hard work to restore himself in the public estimation.

But his sufferings did not end at Santa Fe. The Governor of the Province sent him and his men to Chihuahua, whence, after a long imprisonment and several months of diplomatic intervention, he was escorted to the coast of the Gulf of Mexico and sent home. He redeemed himself by gallant service in the war of 1812, and was killed at the battle of York, in Upper Canada, having been promoted to the rank of Brigadier-General.

At this time Kansas was a part of Indiana, but the Territory of Missouri was created in 1812, and in the same year Lieut. Long crossed the plains, having come from Pittsburgh to Independence, Mo., by way of the Ohio, Mississippi and Missouri rivers. He followed Pike's trail over the prairies, and entering the mountains northwest of Denver, discovered the mighty peak which stands as his monument, and spent eight years in exploration, traversing 26,000 miles of prairie and wilderness.

In June, 1842, General Fremont, then a Captain of Engineers, started from Independence on the expedition which brought him so much fame. Kit Carson was his guide, and the party followed what is known as "the Smoky Hill Trail," the present route of the Kansas Pacific Railroad. Fremont found St. Vrains Fort, at the foot of the Rocky Mountains, on the Platte River, near where Denver stands, and after recruiting there awhile, visited Manitou Springs, the Garden of the Gods, and other natural wonders in that vicinity, which had been discovered and described by Pike some thirty years before. Then he pushed into the mountains, climbed several of the loftiest peaks, and in the fall of the same year came home by way of the Santa Fe Trail, stopping for a few days' rest at what was known as Bent's Fort, near where Fort Lyon was afterwards located, a few miles from La Junta.

These two forts, Bent's and St. Vrain's, were trading posts of the Hudson Bay Company, where stockades had been erected for the protection of men and merchandise, and where the Indians and the trappers exchanged buffalo and other skins for beads and blankets, whisky and powder. St. Vrain was a French Canadian, and Bent was a Missourian who had been a hunter and trapper from boyhood.

The subsequent year Fremont started out again, with a wider purpose, better equipped, and accompanied by a larger force of men. He had a grand scheme of exploration, including the whole Western Continent, from the Arctic Seas to the Gulf of California. So ambitious, so enthusiastic was he, that he awakened the suspicions of the public lest he might have some ulterior design, and the fact that he took a little brass mountain howitzer with him was cited to prove that he meant carnage and conquest. The doctrine of "manifest destiny" was being agitated, and the invasion and annexation of Mexico was discussed in every school-house debating society and every corner grocery in the land. A mountain was made out of a mole-hill, and in deference to the popular demand, the Secretary of War sent a message after Fremont ordering him to abandon his expedition and return to Washington.

Here fate, as has often been the case, was outwitted by a woman. The order reached St. Louis, where Fremont had been outfitting, on the day of his departure, and the envelope was opened by his brilliant and beautiful wife, the daughter of Senator Thomas H. Benton, who in the presidential campaign of 1856 was an active and influential partner in the firm of "Fremont and Jessie." She realized that it was a crisis in her husband's career, and had the courage to tuck the order of the Government into her pocket. Fremont started out as he had originally planned, and the expedition, which but for a woman's presence of mind would have been abandoned, made him a hero, a General, a Senator, and a candidate for the Presidency.

Fremont is commonly supposed to have been the

first man to cross the continent to California, as Lewis and Clarke were the first to see the Western Ocean from the rock-ribbed coast of Oregon, but it is a mistake. Sylvester Pattie, a Virginian, with his son and a party of five other men, made the journey eighteen years before Fremont started, and is believed to deserve the honor. Before Pattie's time, the Pacific Ocean was seen by hunters and trappers, although to Fremont's energy and skill the world owes the first maps and technical knowledge it received of California. Pattie left the Missouri River on the 20th of June, 1824, joining General Pratt's trading party for Santa Fe, of which he was made commander. They reached Santa Fe without adventure; but the night after they arrived a courier came in, announcing that the Comanche Indians had attacked a settlement on the Pecos River, had murdered a number of people, and carried off several women as prisoners. The Governor asked Pattie if his men would assist in the pursuit, and they cheerfully complied. The next day the Indians were cut off in their retreat, and when Pattie's command came upon them, they witnessed a sight that almost froze their blood.

In front of a column of mounted Indian warriors walked five women, stark naked, while their cruel captors occasionally lashed them with their whips. Their feet were lacerated by sharp stones, and were filled with the poisonous barbs of the cactus. What they had suffered cannot be described. They were all young ladies of high social standing and education, and one of them, Jovaca, was a daughter of an

Ex-Governor of New Mexico. She is described as being very beautiful, and just in the blush of womanhood. The sight enraged the chivalrous Americans, and they sprang upon the Indians from their ambush. Three of the women were immediately slaughtered by the savages, to prevent their escape or rescue, but Jovaca and one other were saved. The Indians fled; and Jovaca with her companion joyfully welcomed their deliverers, blankets and other clothing being found for them to wear. On their return to Santa Fe, the father of Jovaca was met, and wept tears of gratitude upon the breast of the brave American. Finishing their business at Santa Fe, Pattie and five of his party accompanied the father to his home at Albuquerque, where they remained for some time, and then started on a hunting expedition to Arizona.

Upon Pattie's return, he passed the winter with the old gentleman, and subsequently took charge of some copper mines in the neighborhood. Three years were spent there, when Pattie returned to his hunting ground. He went down the Gila River to where it joins the Colorado, and finally reached some Spanish settlements in California, where his party had a severe experience, being arrested as spies and kept in prison for some time. They finally secured their release and took a vessel from San Diego for Vera Cruz. During his hunting in California, Pattie went to San Francisco, which was then a Spanish Catholic mission, thus being the first white man to make an overland passage from the Eastern States to the harbor of the Golden Gate, which was afterwards to occupy such a prominent place upon the map of the world.

In 1858, the first party of miners for Pike's Peak, a dozen Kansas men, passed over "the Smoky Hill trail," and were followed during that year and the two succeeding years by thousands of people, with the familiar legend, "Pike's Peak or Bust," painted upon the sides of their canvas wagon covers.

On the 23d of January, 1859, the first railroad train reached the Missouri River over the Hannibal and St. Joe, and just a year later, lacking one day, the first iron rail was laid in Kansas soil on what was then known as the Ellwood and Marysville road. April 13th, 1860, the famous pony express, carrying the mails between St. Joseph and San Francisco, was inaugurated, and in 1866 the Kansas Pacific Railroad was commenced.

In 1861, Kansas was admitted to the Union as a State, and in 1863 Congress voted a grant of land along the Arkansas River to the Atchison, Topeka & Santa Fe Railroad Company. A survey was made, which resulted in the adoption of the old Santa Fe Trail as the route. This trail, of which a history is given in the next chapter, was the longest road on the globe, and in some respects the most remarkable. It was originally travelled by the buffalo, which Baron von Humboldt said was the best civil engineer in the world. Thomas H. Benton, in a speech in the Senate, quoted Humboldt's remark, and called attention to the fact that the best roads in America were those that traversed the trail of the bison. The Indian was his first follower, then the pioneer with his wagon, and then the railway engineer with his iron track. This is true in Pennsylvania and Virginia, Kentucky, and everywhere the animal has been. It was strikingly illustrated by the experience of the engineers who laid the track of the Baltimore & Ohio Railroad through Cumberland Gap. They tried to find a better line than that the buffalo had laid out for them, and expended hundreds of thousands of dollars in attempting shorter distances and better grades through the mountains, but were finally compelled to abandon them all and adopt the survey the instincts of the oldest inhabitant had discovered.

In February, 1867, forty miles of the A., T. & S. F. Railroad were in operation; in 1870 it was completed to Emporia, and in 1873 was pushed through to the Colorado line. The panic of that year suspended operations, but they were resumed in 1877, and the road was completed to a connection with the Southern Pacific at Deming, in 1881. The line follows the old trail from Topeka to Santa Fe, almost every mile having its legends of romantic and historical interest.

CHAPTER II.

STORIES OF THE OLD SANTA FE TRAIL.

EARLY in the century fables of the riches and splendors of the Spanish Hidalgos of New Mexico began to reach the ears of the frontier traders, and they came to believe that across the southwestern boundary, which was then the lower line of Kansas and Colorado, lay a market that was unsurpassed. The Spanish rulers were supposed to be rolling in luxury and given to boundless extravagance, and the return of Lieut. Pike from his long pilgrimage and hazardous adventures, gave the theories the substance of fact. In 1804, a French creole by the name of La Lande, started from Kaskaskia, Ill., for Santa Fe, with several pack mules laden with goods, belonging to a trader named Morrison, but he never returned, and was thought to have been killed by the Indians.

In 1812, four men, inspired by Lieut. Pike's reports, thought they would try to make their way through, and started from Booneville with a pack train laden with merchandise. The names of three of these bold adventurers were McKnight, Beard and Chambers, but the fourth is lost to tradition. They followed Pike's trail to the foot of the mountains, along the Arkansas River, and then took a southerly course, arriving at Santa Fe without any exciting experience. This was the first endeavor to establish trade with the Spanish settlements, and proved disastrous, for upon their arrival at the capital of New Mexico, the excitement over Pike's arrest was revived. They were thrown into prison as spies, their goods were confiscated and they narrowly escaped execution.

They found at Santa Fe, upon their arrival, the man La Lande, who was supposed to have been lost, but who went through safely, set himself up as a merchant with the capital that belonged to Morrison, his employer, and was living in luxury with a Mexican wife. The only American there was James Pursley, the first emigrant to New Mexico from the United States. Pursley was a trapper, and while following his trade along the foot hills of the Rocky Mountains, had fallen in with some Indians who told him of the Spanish settlements a few hundred miles below. He decided make them a visit, and went first to Taos, a pueblo or village seventy miles north of Santa Fe on the Rio Grande River, and then to the capital, where he took up a permanent residence, married a Mexican woman and kept a miserable hotel until his death, twenty-four years afterward. He was the only American to welcome the gallant Pike when the latter arrived at Santa Fe as a prisoner, and acted as interpreter during his interviews with the authorities.

McKnight and his companions were kept in prison nine years, until the revolution of 1821, led by Iturbide, when they were released, and returned to Missouri in a canoe down the Arkansas River. Nothing daunted by his perilous experience, in the following year (1822) Mr. Beard, of the McKnight party, induced some capitalists of St. Louis to furnish the means for another experiment, and he started again, with a small party, and several thousand dollars' worth of merchandise laden upon pack-horses. They reached a point near La Junta in safety, but were there overtaken by a violent snow storm, and driven into the timber of an island in the Arkansas River for shelter. A rigorous winter followed, and they were compelled to build huts for protection and remain there for three long months. Some of the party perished from exposure and the rest nearly died of starvation. They were compelled to kill their horses for food, and spring found them with a valuable cargo of merchandise upon their hands with no means of transportation. In this emergency they made a *cache*, a term used by Canadian voyagers to describe a place of concealment, and digging deep pits on the bank of the river, buried their goods and started on foot over the mountains. They reached Taos in safety, obtained some mules and returned for their buried property, which was taken to Santa Fe and sold at an enormous profit.

The mossy pits where Beard buried his goods lie near Las Animas, very close to the boundary line between Colorado and New Mexico, and are still pointed out by ranchmen who ride over that country after the roaming cattle.

When these traders reached Santa Fe the haughty and insolent Hidalgos, who had ruled the country commercially, as well as politically and socially, so long, endeavored to dispose of them as McKnight and his party had been treated, but there was a new and more liberal administration since the revolution, which was inclined to encourage competition and welcome commerce; so the Santa Fe trade began. The profits of the expedition were enormous, and Beard's party returned to Missouri with their pack-mules laden with wool and gold and silver and turquois, for which they had exchanged their merchandise. Up to this date the New Mexicans had obtained all of their supplies from Spain by vessel to Vera Cruz, whence they were transported at great cost across the country, and were sold at exorbitant prices. Calicos that could be purchased in Missouri for a sixpence a yard, cost two or three dollars at Santa Fe, and cutlery was in demand at almost any price.

A man named Captain Becknall was the next trader to start out, and he left Missouri in 1822 with four companions and a stock of goods to trade with the Indians for furs. He met Beard's returning party, and learning of thir success with the Mexicans, went to Santa Fe instead, bringing back large profits to Booneville. Then Col. Cooper went out in May, 1822, with a party of fifteen men and several thousand dollars' worth of merchandise, which he exchanged at Taos for silver ornaments, wool and skins.

The same year Captain Becknall made a second trip, but, however, with different results. Having great confidence in his ability to find a shorter route to Santa Fe, the captain left his old trail and started across the country, to avoid the circuitous valley of the river. It was a fatal mistake, as the party found themselves in a sandy desert without any water supply, and wandered about for several days enduring sufferings that pass description. They killed their dogs, and cut off the ears of their mules in the vain hope of assuaging their thirst with the hot blood. Several of the men died, while the others pushed on with parched throats and burning flesh, following the cruel mirage of the prairie which has lured so many to destruction. The strongest of the party were just fainting with fatigue, and would soon have perished but for a buffalo that came upon them. They shot him for his blood, and found his stomach distended with water. This filthy liquid saved their lives, and they followed the track of the animal to a creek at which he had just been drinking.

The profits of the trade with Santa Fe were so large as to enlist in it merchants of capital, and parties started from Booneville nearly every month during the summer. In 1824 the trade became so large that wagons were introduced, and the first wheels passed over the prairie in May of that year. The famous General Marmaduke, afterward Lieutenant Governor of Missouri, and later a confederate leader, was one of the party. The first caravan reached Santa Fe without any difficulties, and the light wagons were a great curiosity to the New Mexicans, who had never seen anything better than the clumsy ox carts used by the native farmers.

So rapidly did train follow train that in 1825 the Hon. Thomas H. Benton secured from congress an appropriation of $25,000 for "the survey and improvement of a wagon road from the Missouri River to the New Mexican boundary," and under this authority Major Sibley, of the United States army, laid out what has since passed into the history of the frontier as the Santa Fe Trail, the longest, and in many respects the most remarkable, road in the world, 800 miles in length, without a bridge from end to end, and rising almost imperceptibly from an elevation of only 500 feet to a height of over 8,000 above the sea. The eastern terminus was orginally at Booneville, then at Independence, then at St. Joseph, Mo., receding as civilization advanced, at first very slowly, but afterward with great rapidity, when the railroad commenced to stretch itself out across the plains.

At one time there were as many as four thousand people engaged in the Santa Fe trade, and a capital of several millions of dollars was employed in its transactions. The traders would start from different points along the river, where the freight had been transferred from steamboats to the wagons, and rendezvous at Council Grove, a long piece of timber on the bank of the Kansas, or Kaw river, near the present site of Emporia. Here the several parties would come together and organize for the long march. A captain of the caravan was elected, every wagon having one vote, and there used to be lively contests for the choice. The idea of such organization was to secure better protection from the Indians, and the trains that exercised the usual precautions were seldom attacked. They were generally composed of three or four hundred wagons, often carrying half a million dollars worth of property, with about three men to every two wagons. A small cannon was commonly carried, as that was more effective in Indian warfare than a hundred muskets, and a regular system of guards and pickets was maintained. Very often the wives and families of traders accompanied them upon the prairie voyage, and it became a favorite journey of tourists and invalids.

The captain of the caravan was chosen for his ability in leadership, and his executive talent. The office was no sinecure and few men could properly fill it. The captain was an autocrat. His revolver was his scepter, and he would shoot a man down for a breach of discipline with as little remorse as he would kill a disabled mule. The teamsters, "mule-whackers," "bull-whackers," or "cow-punchers," as they were variously called, were not a gentle or a diffident class of men, and safety required the strictest discipline. Each man had his duties to perform, and any dispute was decided by the captain, from whose decision there was no appeal. If a member of the party was dissatisfied with the captain's government he could leave the caravan and take the journey alone, but if he remained he must obey.

Guides and scouts were always employed to look after camping places, at which the three essentials, water, fuel and grass, must be found; to hunt game for the food of the expedition, and to watch for Indian signs. This was the business of Kit Carson, the most remarkable and the ablest plainsman this country has produced, whose name is associated with almost every step of progress in the Southwest.

The caravan used to follow its weary path in a long and lazy procession, four wagons abreast, and the traveler along the Atchison, Topeka & Santa Fe Railroad can see even to-day, where the plow has not turned the sod, the deep ruts that were made in the soft soil by the wagon wheels. At night the wagons were formed in a hollow square, with their tongues out, making a safe and sheltered pen for the animals. Each party camped outside its own wagons, and every man stood his turn on guard. With these precautions the long journey across the plains was not attended with much hazard, and very seldom was one of the large trains attacked. The Indians confined their depredations to small and reckless parties, and disaster only followed carelessness. Kit Carson left on record his opinion that whisky has killed more men on the frontier than the Indians, and there is no doubt of the fact. But ignorance of Indian customs, and foolhardy recklessness have caused the sacrifice of many lives and much property. Persons who were "wise in their own conceit" very frequently thought they could shorten the route by leaving the trail and "cutting across lots," but invariably came to grief, as in some cases that have already been cited.

In 1833 a party of tourists and traders, of which a brother of General Robert C. Schenck was a member, left the trail to save time and distance, lost their reckoning, exhausted their provisions, and fired away all their ammunition at game. They wandered about for several weeks in the greatest distress, first killing their horses for food, and then feeding upon the leaves and roots of shrubs. The party divided over a difference of opinion as to the proper direction to take, and one branch finally reached an Indian camp, where they were hospitably treated and permitted to return to the states. The others, among whom was Mr. Schenck, were never seen alive again, but months afterwards their bones were found, and identified by some articles of clothing, as they lay bleaching upon the prairie.

The lack of water in the summer season constituted the greatest danger. The western plains of Kansas were once the bottom of a great lake, whose waves dashed against the Rocky Mountains. At the time when what geologists call "the great continental elevation" took place, the lake was raised above the sea level, and the vast area of water was gradually diminished by drainage until nothing but ponds were left in the natural depressions, and the streams that carry the melting snows of the mountains to the sea. The contents of the ponds were lapped up by the winds and the sun, the sands of their bottoms hardened into rock, and made a mighty sarcophagus for the beasts, and birds, and fishes, and insects that were the original inhabitants. From a sea of water the plains became a great earth ocean, and on every side the waves of buffalo grass roll up against the shores of the horizon. Where were once billows of water are now billows of sand, over which in years past the white fleets of prairie schooners used to encounter more cruel dangers than were ever confronted upon the sea. Savages and soldiers, battles and hunts, hunger and thirst, murder, fire and rapine, have made long cemeteries of the two trails across the continent, one leading to the treasure store houses of the Rocky Mountains and the other to the legendary land of Montezuma.

When the traders approached Santa Fe, rapid riders would be sent ahead to make contracts and engage warehouses, and the arrival of a caravan made a holiday in the quaint old Spanish town. Having sold their goods for Spanish dollars, or exchanged them for silver or turquois, the traders would spend several weeks in carousal, lose much of their money in the gambling houses, and then reload their wagons with wool and start on the homeward journey.

At that time New Mexico belonged to Spain, and a heavy tariff was imposed upon all foreign traders, amounting sometimes to two and three hundred per cent. The customs officers were very corrupt, and it is believed that little of the money they collected ever reached the coffers of the government. For a few years Gov. Armijo maintained a tariff of his own, exacting five hundred dollars for each wagon load, and those who paid this cheerfully are said to have easily escaped the other imposts.

In 1839, when all the Mexican seaports were blockaded by the French, the Santa Fe trade reached enormous proportions, as it was the only means Old Mexico as well as New Mexico had of securing supplies, but in 1843, during the war between Texas and Mexico, it was suspended entirely, Santa Anna issuing a decree forbidding the importation of goods from the North and closing the custom houses. The trail was opened again in 1846, however, when General Kearney captured Santa Fe and planted the

Stars and Stripes upon the ancient mud "palace" of the haughty Dons. Business increased, a stage line was established, and finally the railroads began to reach toward the Southwest with their iron arms. The forwarding houses kept advancing with the track, first to Emporia, then to Larnard, Fort Dodge, La Junta and Los Vegas. The railroad track follows the old trail very closely, and the journey that was once five weeks long, is now a scamper of only three days.

CHAPTER III.

ARMY AND INDIAN LIFE ON THE BORDER.

IN 1825, when the Old Santa Fe Trail was surveyed under an act of Congress, three Government Commissioners, Messrs. Sibley, Reeves and Mathews, met the Indians at Council Grove, near Emporia, and gave them $800 worth of beads and blankets and gewgaws, in consideration of which they agreed not to molest travellers across the plains. How well they kept their promise the bloody trails and bleached bones upon the prairie testify.

The aboriginal owners of Kansas were the Pawnee Indians, at one time the most powerful of all the prairie tribes, but now reduced by war and disease to utter insignificance. At one time, it is said, they could muster 25,000 warriors, but in a single year the small-pox swept away more than half their number, and then the combined strength of their heriditary enemies, the Sioux, the Cheyennes, Comanches, and Kiowas, easily conquered them.

The scanty remnant of the great Delaware race, made famous by Cooper's novels, found their final home in Kansas, and have been used by the Government as scouts in the many Indian wars. They were once a mighty nation, living in Pennsylvania, New Jersey and Southern New York, but are now but a few hundreds hastening to extinction. In 1700 they were moved to the Valley of the Susquehanna, in 1751 to Muskingham County, Ohio, in 1781 to Sandusky, in 1812 to the Whitewater of Indiana, and in 1829 to Camp Leavenworth, which was the first fort established in Kansas, and is now the headquarters of the Commander of the Military Department. In 1829 Fort Riley was established, four miles below Junction City and fifty miles northwest of Emporia. It is the geographical center of the United States, the exact spot being marked by a shaft of masonry.

In 1846, the first grand march of the army was made across the continent, along the very line the railroad follows to-day, by that gallant soldier, Stephen W. Kearney, each day's progress being noted in the afterwards published diary of General W. H. Emory, then a Lieutenant of Engineers. The army crossed the Raton Mountains where the railroad engineers found the easiest grade up that steep and rocky range, being obliged to draw the wagons over the mountain sides by long ropes, with which hundreds of soldiers assisted the helpless mules. It was supposed that Armijo, the Mexican Governor, would resist the entrance of the army into Santa Fe, but Kearney took possession of the capital without firing a single shot.

From that time on a large part of the army was engaged in protecting the trail from the ravages of the Indians, and several forts were built along its line, at Larnard, Dodge, Las Animas, and other places, but they are all abandoned now, except old

Fort Union, near Watrous, New Mexico, where a small garrison is kept as a protection for the cattle ranges against the tribes in Indian Territory.

A few miles west of Larnard is a little settlement called Pawnee Rock, which stands upon a spot that is rich in history and Indian tradition. South of the track a few miles can be seen a huge pile of sand stone rising from the prairie that makes a conspicuous landmark and can be seen for many miles. It is not so large as it once was, for the settlers having more need of building material than reverence for Indian traditions, have blasted and carted a large portion of it away. The landmark is still quite noticeable, however, and can be easily seen from the cars. It has been known as Pawnee Rock since any place in this country had a name, and for centuries has been the rendezvous and camping ground of the Indians. All over its weather-beaten front are carved the names of hundreds of people who have passed over the Santa Fe Trail during the last sixty years, and among them is still discernible that of Robert E. Lee, who went to Mexico with the expedition of 1846 as a captain in the Mounted Rifles.

The old trail passes under the shadow of the Rock, and if this mighty sentinel could speak, it would tell of desperate adventures and tragic events that have taken place around it. There are old and almost obliterated trails leading in every direction from the great spring near by, at which all the famous Indians and scouts and soldiers that have traversed these plains have found refreshment. It was the favorite camping and resting place of the traders as well as the Indians, but was considered the most dangerous point on the entire journey. Almost every rod of turf for miles around covers a grave, and the early settlers often resurrected the bones of those who have died in its tragedies.

A few years ago a farmer near by ploughed up the graves of two men, and near the bones were found pieces of flat stone on which two names were carved. Col. Henry Inman, of Kansas, took some trouble to investigate the matter, and found that the bones were those of two trappers, named Boyd and Thorpe, who were killed by the Indians while on their way to the States with a cargo of skins.

The first Indian fight in which Kit Carson ever engaged took place at Pawnee Rock, in the spring of '33. Kit was a mere boy then, only seventeen years old, and was hired by Col. St. Vrain, an agent of the Hudson Bay Company, to accompany his party west, to drive animals and make himself generally useful. When the party reached Pawnee Rock they saw Indian signs, and had scarcely made camp, when they were attacked, but they dispersed the Indians without suffering any damage. There was a good deal of nervousness among the men, and young Kit, while on guard, fired his gun at what he supposed was an Indian, and shot his own mule through the head. But the next morning he had plenty of Indians to shoot at, for the Pawness attacked them, and kept up the fight for several days.

Kit never tired of telling this story, but he had another one that he used to tell, about how Jim Gibson and "his partner" were forced to "run-a-muck" by the Kiowa Indians in 1836. Bill was the partner's name, and they were on their way back to the States from a trapping expedition. They met a large party of Indians at the Rock, and ran up to the top of it to escape them. Here they were treed, but succeeded in hiding their mules in the crevices of the Rock, and got sufficient protection for themselves to hold the Indians at bay. They were charged and charged again, but always succeeded in driving the Indians back, killing about thirty of the band; but their ammunition finally gave out, and they had a parley with the Indians. O-ton-son-e-var—the chief—proposed that one of them should run the knife gauntlet, two hundred paces, and finally agreed that if he escaped with his life, both might go free. Bill was an active man and a splendid runner. He stripped to his drawers, and when the signal was given, darted through the double row of savages, with their knives drawn, like a flash of lightning. Not a knife touched him, and he and Jim Gibson, his partner, were allowed to go free.

In the river near Larned is a little island, covered with willows, cottonwoods and box elders. At this place there once occurred a terrific fight between a band of Pawnees and a band of Cheyennes under the command of Yellow Buffalo, one of the bravest and handsomest Indians that ever trod the plains. The Pawnees on the island sent a challenge to the Cheyennes, who were their hereditary enemies, and the defiance was responded to promptly by Yellow Buffalo. He fought them all day, and at night sent for reinforcements, which came from the main camp, with the famous chief, Black Kettle, who afterwards gave Gen. Sheridan so much trouble, at their head. The fight was renewed in the morning, and continued all day. The Pawnees on the island, although outnumbered ten to one, held their ground bravely, until the Cheyennes were compelled to withdraw.

In 1866 and 1867, the Indians carried on a relentless warfare against the settlements of the frontier, and almost stopped the trade with Santa Fe. The whole frontier, from Wyoming to Texas, was swept over again and again by marauding bands of Cheyennes, Kiowas and Arapahoes, and General Hancock, who was commanding the Department, undertook to punish and suppress them. The Indians were so bold that they committed depredations and captured stragglers under the very shadows of the forts; attacked emigrant camps and trains of traders, burned the dwellings and stole the stock of the frontier ranchemen, killing the men and taking the women into a captivity that was worse than death. A trooper from Fort Dodge was out hunting one day, and being captured alive by the savages, was tortured in the most horrible manner. He was stripped naked, tied to a stake, strips of flesh were cut from his body, arms and legs, and burning brands thrust into the bleeding wounds; his nose, ears, lips, fingers and toes were cut off one by one, until he died from suffering and loss of blood.

Two young officers of the Seventh Cavalry went out from Fort Dodge one day to take a swim in the river, and while floundering around in the refreshing water like a couple of porpoises, were discovered by the Indians sneaking among the neighboring hilltops, waiting an opportunity to take the scalp of some poor straggler. The officers detected the Indians soon enough to escape, but not in time to make their toilets, and the inhabitants of the post were astonished to see them riding toward home like a couple of naked madmen, closely pursued by a band of howling savages. They were so glad to get back alive that they were not regretful at the loss of their clothes, watches and pocket-books.

In 1867, General Hancock held a very important council with the Cheyenne, Kiowa, Arapahoe and Comanche Indians at Pawnee Rock, the principal chiefs of all the tribes being present. The object of the council was to secure the peace of the frontier by treaty instead of war. Several white women and children were in the hands of the Indians as captives, and it was hoped that negotiations could effect their release, and the surrender of those savages who had been concerned in repeated massacres. On the morning of the day on which the council was to be held, General Hancock, followed by his staff and troops, rode up to the appointed place, and witnessed one of the most imposing displays of savage warfare that was ever beheld. The immense bodies of warriors were bedecked in their brightest paint, wore their most gorgeous costumes, their heads crowned with brilliant war bonnets, their lances glistening in the sun, their bows strung, and their quivers full of barbed arrows; in addition to this, each had a breech-loading rifle, which had been provided by the wise forethought and tender solicitude of the Government. On the other hand was Gen. Hancock, with his staff, at the head of a column of about fifteen hundred regulars, presenting a contrast that was very striking. There, in battle array, a few rods from each other, were two large bodies of men, representing the civilized and barbarous modes of warfare. As the chiefs met, Gen. Hancock told them that if war was their object, he was ready to begin it then and there. Their immediate answer was that they did not desire war, but that their hearts were good toward the whites, and they wanted peace. The council was postponed, at the request of the Indians, until the next day. During the night it was reported that the Indians were preparing to leave. Gen. Custer made an attack upon their camp, and found it empty, except for one living soul, and that a little half-breed girl, who had been forgotten. The display of strength before holding the council was to intimidate the troops, and not being successful at that, their postponement was merely a ruse to gain time to retreat.

A few months afterward, Gen. Hancock had another council with the same Indians, at Fort Dodge, during which they made extravagant promises of future good conduct, and so persuasive was the oratory of Santanta, the famous Kiowa chief, that Gen. Hancock presented him with a Major-General's dress-coat, sash and epaulettes. In return for this compliment, Santanta a few weeks after attacked Fort Dodge, arrayed in his new uniform, and succeeded in stealing nearly all the government horses and cattle quartered there.

The condition of the frontier grew worse instead of better, and during the summer of 1868, according to the official reports, 154 white people were killed by the Indians, 16 were wounded, 14 women were outraged, 24 children carried into captivity, 669 horses and over 1,000 cattle stolen, 14 houses burned and 11 stage coaches attacked. It became a matter of national alarm, emigration ceased, the railroads stopped work, and the settlers began to leave the state. Hancock's campaign having been an expensive failure, General Sheridan concluded, as he remarked, "to take a hand in the fuss himself." In September, 1868, he moved his headquarters to Fort Hayes, on the extreme frontier, and began preparations for a winter campaign, which was at the time unprecedented; but its success demonstrated the advantages to the white man of fighting Indians in the winter, when they can secure but little food for their ponies, and are impeded in their movements by their squaws and papooses, who generally follow the war parties. The great disadvantage which the regular army suffers in Indian warfare is the inability of the regular soldier, and particularly his horse, to travel as far and as fast as the ponies of the savages can go without food and water. The Indian carries no supplies but a little jerked buffalo meat hung to his saddle, and depends largely upon plunder for subsistence. The trooper is impeded by heavy trappings and long wagon trains, carrying his rations and his baggage. When the two bodies finally come in contact, civilization always wins, except against overwhelming odds, and the savage knows it; so his system of warfare is to harass the troops, stampede their animals and cut off small bodies of soldiers who sometimes become separated from the main column.

In order to overcome some of these difficulties, and have a force at hand that could excel the Indians in speed and endurance, General Sheridan organized a company of scouts, numbering fifty picked men, every one of whom was famous for courage, endurance, and knowledge of Indian character. They were all frontiersmen, and were gathered from the settlements of Kansas, and the hunting camps. Some of them were desperate adventurers of the Wild Bill type, to whom fighting was a pastime; others were trappers and hunters, guides, and professional scouts, and more were ranchmen, who had seen their families murdered, their houses burned and their stock stolen by the same Indians they expected to encounter. They were not fighting for pay, nor for glory, but for the love of it, or to satisfy their thirst for revenge. They wore no uniform, but each was dressed as he came from his ranche, carrying his own rifle, and riding his own grass-fed mustang. They carried no baggage but their blankets and bullets, and no rations but a little coffee and hardtack, expecting to kill game for food as they went. This motley and desperate gang of men was probably the most formidable body for its size that the redskins ever encountered, as they subsequently discovered. Not one among the fifty knew the definition of fear, and what would be hardship and exposure to other men was luxury to them.

To command this company required genius as well as nerve, courage and endurance. It must be a man who would receive their respect and enforce discipline. George A. Forsythe, an *aid-de-camp* to General Sheridan, was selected as possessing, above all others, the necessary qualifications. At the outbreak of the rebellion Forsythe was a clerk in the drygoods house of John V. Farwell & Co., at Chicago. He was one of the first men to enlist, and was twice rejected because of his age and slight physique, being but a mere stripling. But persistence got him into the army, and courage and military skill secured his promotion, until he finally attracted the attention of General Sheridan who gave him a place on his staff, and kept him there until 1882, when Forsythe was called to the command of the Fourth Cavalry, at Fort Cummings, New Mexico.

Besides this company of frontiersmen, Sheridan had the famous Seventh Cavalry, under General Custer, the Fifth and Third Regiments of infantry, and a battalion of Pawnee and Osage Indian scouts, thirsting for the blood of the Cheyennes, Kiowas and Arapahoes, their ancient enemies.

Forsythe's scouts were called into action before the command was ready to move. A government wagon train was boldly raided and captured by the Indians in the very vicinity of the Fort, and Forsythe started out to intercept their retreat. He followed their trail closely, and the second night out bivouaced on a little island of sand, in what is known as the Arrikaree fork of the Republican River. The scouts were exhausted and slept like logs on the ground, but the first man who awoke next morning shouted:

"Great God! General, look at the Injuns."

And well might he be astonished, for during the night the camp had been entirely surrounded by thousands of savages. The odds were about fifty to one, but the little band never quailed for an instant. They did not know exactly how they were going to get out of the scrape, but they did not propose to be scared. The Indians leisurely observed what they believed was to be easy prey; but the scouts lost no time. They dug rifle pits in the sand with their hands and knives and tin coffee cups, ate a comfortable breakfast—the last one they were to have for some time—and calmly awaited the attack. It was not long in coming, and down from the tops of the low hills that surrounded the little valley, under the command of the famous chief, Roman Nose, came, like an avalanche of demons, thousands of hideously-painted savages, in all the glory of their barbarous adornment, shouting their diabolical war cries. It was a charge that made the very earth tremble. Nothing to equal it was ever seen by a white man's eye. The scouts were lying flat on the sand, with their trusty rifles at their shoulders.

"Keep cool, boys," was Forsythe's quiet command, "wait till they get to the river bank, and then every fellow pick out his man; but don't waste a bullet; we'll need all we've got before we get out o' this."

The avalanche was met by a shower of lead. Forsythe's injunction was observed, and not a bullet was wasted. Fifty plumed warriors fell under the feet of their ponies, and the column staggered. A second volley from the repeating rifles of the scouts mowed down another swathe of savages; and a third sent them scattering back again to the hills, leaving long rows of dead and wounded.

The scouts, too, fared badly. Most of their horses, which had been picketed on the island, were killed, Lieut. Beecher, a nephew of the great Brooklyn preacher, and Forsythe's second in command, was mortally hurt, four of the scouts were killed, and several were badly wounded. Forsythe himself discovered a bullet in his thigh, but there was no one to dress his wound, as the surgeon, Dr. Movers, lay dead on the sand, with his rifle in his hand and his finger on the trigger.

The bodies of the dead horses were drawn around in a circle for breast-works just in time to receive a second charge quite as terrific as the first. The scouts reserved their fire until the Indians were close upon them, and then poured volley after volley into their ranks until they fell back broken, demoralized and dismayed. For four days these attacks were kept up, and each time were repulsed with heavy slaughter among the Indians, and more or less casualties among the scouts. Forsythe had plenty of ammunition, and could secure water when it was wanted by digging in the sand, but he had no food, no opportunity to rest or sleep, and the putrid carcasses of the dead horses made such a stench that the very air was poisoned. Nearly half of the little beleagured band were disabled, either by death or wounds, and the Indians saw, as they themselves realized, that death or surrender was merely a matter of time. The brave men had their choice, and concluded to die. They were nearly all wounded, under the hail of lead that for four days had fallen upon them, and Forsythe not only had his right thigh frightfully lacerated, but the bone of his left leg had been shattered by a bullet. He could not move, but could only lie in his sand pit, behind the festering, bloated body of his horse, and fire his rifle at the savages. There was no opportunity or means for dressing the wounds; no time to cook food if they had any, and the only resort that lay between them and starvation was to cut chunks of rotten, putrid flesh from the haunches of the dead horses and force that down their throats.

The Indians apparently concluded to let the scouts starve in peace, as their attacks had resulted so disastrously, and at noon of the fourth day suspended active hostilities. That night Forsythe asked if any member of the band was willing to undertake the hazardous attempt of going through the Indian village to seek rescue. Two men, an old French scout named Trudeau, and a young man named Stillwell, formerly from Illinois, volunteered. It was a most perilous and almost hopeless mission, and the chances were only one in a thousand of success. That one chance lay in the hope that the Indians might be so confident of their overwhelming numbers, and of the impossibility of the escape of the scouts, as to be indifferent as to what was going on around them. It proved to be well founded, and the two intrepid men crept through the Indian lines, almost stepping upon the bodies of the sleeping savages. They reached the fort safely and handed to the astonished commander a ragged and crumpled piece of paper, torn from Forsythe's note book, on which was scrawled in pencil these mild words:

"I am on a little island and have plenty of ammunition.

" We are living on horse meat, but are entirely out of rations.

" If it were not for so many wounded I would come out and take the chances of getting through. They are evidently sick of their bargain.

"I can hold out six days longer if absolutely necessary, but please lose no time. FORSYTHE."

This little message gave no idea of the situation, but the scouts related, in hurried words, the story Forsythe was too modest and too brave to tell. The bugle sounded "boots and saddles," and Col. Carpenter, at the head of a column of cavalrymen, was soon galloping across the prairie to the rescue.

With what anguish and anxiety and suffering Forsythe and his men awaited the result of the perilous trip of the two scouts cannot be described. He had no means of knowing whether they got through safely, and could only fight and wait. The wounded scouts were dying around him and the dead bodies were decomposing. His own wounds were painful in the extreme, and he could not move the lower part of his body. He could only use his hands to cut off his daily rations of rotten horse flesh, and load and fire his rifle, which he did with effect as often as a charge was made. On the morning of the seventh day there was an unusual commotion among the Indians, and what it meant the scouts did not know. It was soon apparent, however, that the Indians were attacked in the rear, and a column of cavalry in blue came charging through the Indian camp on foaming horses. The weak, starved, and almost exhausted little band on the island raised a feeble cheer, which was responded to by their rescuers. The Indians fled at once, and when Colonel Carpenter reached the little island he found Forsythe pretending to read an old novel he carried in his saddle bags.

The indifference of the rescued was not well disguised, however, and Forsythe finally admitted that he was never so glad to meet any one in his life as he was when Col. Carpenter came to him on the banks of the Arrikaree.

General Sheridan took the field in person, and the war was kept up all winter with Fort Dodge as the base of operations. Early in November two scouts were sent by General Sheridan from his camp with important dispatches for Fort Dodge. One was McDonald, a half breed, the son of an old Scotch trapper and his Indian wife, the other was an Ohio boy named Davis, who, attracted by General Fremont's fascinating description of life on the plains, left his home at an early age and spent his life on the frontier. The scouts had a ride of a hundred miles through a country swarming with Indians, but they accepted their duty with cheerful and fearless determination. They never reached Fort Dodge, however, and several weeks after their bodies were found under a tree that was almost cut down by the bullets that had passed through it. They had been discovered by the Indians and made a gallant defense, dying only when their ammunition was exhausted.

The campaign was ended by General Custer's celebrated fight at Witchita, the Indians were driven upon their reservations, and have since given very little trouble to Kansas.

CHAPTER IV.

HEROES OF THE OLD SANTA FE TRAIL.

DANGER always develops heroes, as it develops reck lessness and ruffianism, and a disregard for the value of human life that is almost incredible. But in the countless numbers of hunters, trappers, guides and scouts whose adventures are a part of the history of the Santa Fe Trail, there were some characters who deserve more than a passing glance from the eyes of the denizens of the civilized world. For courage, nerve, endurance, intelligence and manliness, Kit Carson stands at the head of the class he so honorably represented. His biography has been repeatedly written, and his public services have been extensively extolled, but too much cannot be said in praise of his virtues as a man, and his abilities as a frontiersman. If he had been permitted to enjoy the ordinary advantages and associations of civilized life he would have stood among the world's leaders, but he made the most of his privilges, and was the greatest among men of his type and occupation.

The Kit Carson of the imagination was a sort of Wild Bill, a frontier Hercules with a dozen revolvers at his belt, an enormous beard, the swagger of a Pirate King, and a voice like that of a roused lion. The actual Kit Carson was a plain, simple, quiet, silent, unobtrusive man, below medium height, slender in physique, of fair complexion, with a small hand and foot, a pleasant face, curly brown hair, a clear hazel eye, little or no beard, a soft voice, and manners as gentle as a woman's. He was the hero of a hundred desperate adventures, killed more Indians than he could possibly remember, guided more important expeditions than any other man ever did, rescued many people from a captivity that was worse than slavery, and had a better knowledge of plainscraft than any of his contemporaries or successors; but for all this was no boaster, was indifferent to popularity, avoided notoriety, blushed when praised and wept at the sight of human suffering. It is truly said of him that he never had a quarrel on his own account, and never took the life of a man except in self defence or as a measure of justice. He was not a profane man, and was strictly temperate, nor had he the loose habits that characterize the ordinary frontiersman. The word fear had no meaning for him, and his composure and self-confidence under difficulties was phenomenal. He was a splendid horseman and an unerring shot; his knowledge of Indian character was never surpassed, and every one who had to do with him commended Kit Carson as the ideal scout and the best guide ever upon the plains.

General Fremont says of him: "Carson while traveling scarcely ever spoke, but his keen eye was continually examining the country, and his whole manner was that of a man deeply impressed with a sense of responsibility. He never laughed or joked, even by the camp fire, but was always watchful for the comfort of other people. He ate but twice a day, at morning and night, and was strictly temperate. In an Indian country the mule is the best sentry, and Carson always slept with his mule tied to his saddle. A braver man than Carson perhaps never lived; in fact, I doubt if he ever knew what fear was, but with all this he exerciesd great caution. While arranging his bed for the night, his saddle, which he always used as a pillow, and to which the lariat of his mule was always tied, was disposed in such a way as to form a barricade for his head. His pistols, half cocked, were laid above it, and his trusty rifle reposed beneath the blanket by his side, where it was not only ready for instant service, but perfectly protected from the damp."

Kit Carson was born in Kentucky, but went to Missouri with his parents when a child, when that State was the extreme frontier, and only two or three years after it had been ceded by the French to the United States as a part of Louisiana. His father was a saddler, and Kit learned that trade. When he was about sixteen years old, a party of traders for Santa Fe came along and he joined them, crossing the plains with a score of men, leading a pack mule heavily laden with goods for the Santa Fe market. He did not return with them, however, but went to Toas with a hunter and trapper by the name of Kin Kade, a Spaniard who was very highly educated, and from whom Kit learned the Spanish language, and much other valuable knowledge. His association with Kin Kade was practically all the education he ever received. A few years afterward he joined a party of traders, and returned with them to Missouri, and from that time on until he joined Fremont, in 1842, his life was spent as a guide on the plains, and as a hunter and trapper in the mountains under the direction of the Hudson Bay Company, which had its headquarters in the Rocky Mountains. In their employ he went in charge of parties of men, during each winter, through all the hunting and trapping regions between the Missouri River and the Pacific Ocean, and during the summer he guided trains of traders and emigrants over the plains. He came to know every valley and mountain stream, every spring upon the prairies, and his natural instincts as a scout gave him great value. His adventures have filled volumes, and his name and the incidents of his life are more familiar to school boys than those of some of the Presidents of the United States. He guided Fremont on both of his expeditions, and the two men became fast friends.

During the Mexican war, Fremont made Carson Lieutenant of his battalion of Mountaineers, and in 1846, when it became necessary for the "Path-finder" to send dispatches from California to Washington, he intrusted them to Carson, who carried them through the lands of hostile Indians, and more hostile Mexicans, reaching Washington in good time, where he remained for several weeks, the guest of Senator Thomas H. Benton, the father-in-law of General Fremont. This feat of Carsons was unprecedented, and although his fame was already great, it made him a hero, and he received marked attention from all the distinguished men of the Capitol. Mrs.

Jessie Benton Fremont, who was then the leading belle of Washington, met him at the depot, and escorted the blushing trapper, who had scarcely ever seen the inside of a civilized house, to her own magnificent residence. He was a lion in society during his stay in Washington, under the patronage of Mrs. Fremont, and is said to have won the admiration of all by his native manliness and inborn gentility. President Polk made him a lieutenant in the United States Regular Army, and sent him back across the plains with an escort of cavalry. The jealousy of the army officers at Washington was such that the Senate refused to confirm his appointment, and when Carson learned of it, he dismissed his escort and retired to his home in Toas, where he joined his old chum, Maxwell, and established a ranche on what is now known as the Maxwell grant.

He afterward kept a store at Toas, under the firm name of Maxwell & Carson, but was not adapted to mercantile life, and did not succeed very well, so he returned to sheep raising, and remained on his ranche until the rebellion, when he volunteered as a private, and rose to the command of a Colorado regiment, performing gallant and valuable service for the Union.

After the war, "General" Carson, as he was then called, was appointed agent for the New Mexican Indians, and served in that capacity until his death, making a journey to Washington with a party of Apache chiefs in 1867.

He died in 1868, at Fort Lyon, Colorado, near where Bent's old fort used to be, and across the river from the town of Las Animas, in the 60th year of his age. The cause of his death was traced back to a fall he received eight years before, when his mule slipped and threw him upon a pile of rocks. He was originally buried at Fort Lyon, but his body was afterward removed to the old cemetery near Toas.

The story of the Santa Fe Trail that has been told oftener than any other, is about the famous ride of Frank Aubry from Santa Fe to Independence, Missouri, 780 miles, in five days and sixteen hours, his own beautiful mare, "Nellie," having carried him the first 150 miles without a stop, except for food and water. Aubry was a French Canadian, first a guide, then a trader. Like Kit Carson, he was a man of medium stature and slender proportions, but he had iron nerves, great resolution and indomitable persistence. As a pioneer, guide and trader, he did much that is worthy of mention, but the great feat for which he is remembered, was his famous ride. The circumstances were as follows:

Aubry had gone out early in the spring of 1848, with a large amount of goods to Santa Fe. As the American troops were then in possession of the country, our merchants, relieved from the interference of those unscrupulous plunderers, the Mexican custom-house officers, found increased competition, but greater facilities for their trade. Business was, therefore, "booming," and Aubry found no difficulty in getting rid of his stock at an advance of over 100 per cent upon his original investment. Knowing the favorable state of the market, and the description of merchandise best suited to its wants, he determined to attempt a hitherto unheard-of enterprise, by making a second trip to St. Louis, and bringing out another stock before cold weather should embarass the communications between Santa Fe and the settlements. To accomplish this, Aubry allowed himself but eight days to traverse the whole Santa Fe Trail, most of which was dangerous on account of the Indians. Having laid his plans and announced his scheme, he, with four companions, and a small but carefully selected *caballada*, set out upon their trip. They rode hard, but the leader outstripped his men, and by the time Aubry had reached the "crossing of the Arkansas," which is generally considered about half-way, he found himself, with his last horse given out, alone, and on foot. Nothing daunted, however, he pushed on, and reached Mann's Fort, some fifteen or twenty miles from the ford. Here he procured a remount, and then, without waiting to rest, or scarcely to eat, he once more took the trail. Near Pawnee Fork he was pursued and had a narrow escape from a party of Indians, who followed him to the Creek; but finally he entered the city of Independence, within less than the time he himself had specified. It is said that upon being assisted from the saddle, it was found to be stained with his blood. The entire ride was made without sleep, and it is the most remarkable instance of human endurance on record. He made the trip once before in thirteen days, which was considered wonderful, but on this trial surpassed even his own expectations. Aubry was killed in a saloon fracas at Santa Fe in 1854.

One of the prominent hunters and guides along the old Santa Fe Trail in early days, was Col. A. G. Boone, a grandson of the famous pioneer of Kentucky, who, I believe, is still alive, and living somewhere in Kansas, on the proceeds of his successful Indian trading. He was one of the most accomplished plainsmen in the country, could speak all the Indian languages, and always enjoyed the confidence of the tribes. He could go among them in the midst of a war dance, without fearing the slightest injury, and was very useful from time to time in aiding the rescue of captives.

Another notable character, was John Smith, known as "Uncle John," an old trapper and guide, who figured a great deal in frontier history. He had a remarkable experience, if only the truth were told, but as the old gentleman got along in years, his imagination became more fertile and his tongue more loose, and he spent most of his time in drawing long yarns for the benefit of "tender-feet." He was a perfect guide, and an excellent hunter; was acquainted with every fort of the west, and, as he used to say, had drank out of every spring from the mouth of the Yellowstone to the Red River of the South. One of his characteristics, as described in Col. Inman's charming stories, was never to eat quail, and thereby hung a story. The old man was on the plains at one time, with some of his companions, and was about to shoot at a buffalo, when a little quail lit on the barrel of his gun and obstructed his sight. He shook it off, but it returned again. Just at that moment the party was attacked by the Indians, and the fact that he had a load in his gun saved his life. He always believed that the interference of that quail with his buffalo shooting was a special interposition of Providence.

Some of the eyes that cross these pages perhaps have seen an Indian romance of a wild and gory character called "The Wild Huntress of the Plains," or by a name akin to that, and read the story without suspecting that it was founded upon fact. It is true that there used to be a wild woman roaming over the plains of Kansas not many years ago, riding the most intractable of mustangs, and carrying danger wherever she went. Her eye was black and wild, and glittered like that of a snake, and her long, uncombed hair, which the wind had tangled, floated out behind her as she rode, like a cluster of writhing vipers. She lived in an old dug-out, and ate herbs and roots and the meat of buffalo she killed. The Indians feared her, as they have a superstitious terror of all insane persons, and her presence in the neighborhood of one of their villages was a sufficient reason for immediate and hasty removal. She was known as Crazy Ann, and was formerly the wife of a railroad contractor by the name of Peters, who was killed in the most brutal manner by the Indians before her very eyes. She became a maniac, and for several years roamed on the prairies unrestrained, but was finally taken to an insane asylum, where she died.

While the railroad was pushing out in early days, Newton was a pretty hard town, and its inhabitants were very different from the pious Mennonites who live there to-day. There is always one or more mysterious individuals in these frontier pandemoniums, who somehow preserve their secrets and still retain the regard, if not the respect, of the community. The mystery of Newton was an old man, dwarfish in stature, and deformed, who kept a saloon and gambling house. He had a wonderfully intelligent face, quick, shrewd eyes, and had only two apparent objects in life. One was to accumulate money, for he was a perfect miser, and a handy man at all games of cards; and the other a watchful and tender solicitude for the welfare of his daughter, the only being for whom he ever showed any respect or affection. She was a beautiful girl, bright, intelligent, and apparently loved the crooked old miser. He was educated, and taught her from books, in a building half tent and half shanty, that stood behind his gambling house. She did the cooking, and was seldom seen except when he was with her. Every luxury that could be secured on the inhospitable frontier was seized for the girl by the old man, and the only money he was ever known to expend from the large quantities he gathered in, was for her benefit.

The story went that she was his only child, and that he had come west to make a fortune, in order that when she grew to womanhood she might live like a lady in the States.

Nobody knew where he came from, although he had for several years driven a team and handled some goods of his own on the Santa Fe Trail, nor did any one know his name. He carried a nickname, as every other man of consequence in the community did, and it was derived from his peculiar habitual expression, "Jes-so."

To every remark that was addressed him, to every assertion that was made in his presence, be it a matter of dinner or death, he had only one reply, and that was:

"Jes-so."

The girl was about seventeen, and was so carefully guarded that she was discontented, and used to have sly flirtations with cow-boys and other hangers on at the camp, which would have ended in murder had the old man discovered them. While he was at the card table, she was chatting at the rear of her tent with one of her many lovers. And one night she eloped!

The old man used to gamble all night and sleep all day, and when he awoke one afternoon from his slumbers, he detected her absence. A cow-boy named "Bunny" was also missing, and the old man, by making inquiries, discovered that they had been seen together during the previous evening. He remarked "Jes-so," as usual, but he crawled through the town like a wild-cat, and borrowing a horse, buckled his revolver belt around him, and started across the prairie toward the ranche where "Bunny" was employed.

The next day he returned to Newton, said "Jes-so," as usual, but sold out his traps, and disappeared forever.

Two days later, travellers along the road reported that they had found, in an abandoned mud-hut near the river, two corpses, those of a beautiful girl and a stalwart young man. They were on their knees, their right hands were clasped, and a catholic prayer-book, covered with blood, lay on the floor beside them. The old man had discovered the betrayal of his daughter by "Bunny," had married them, according to the catholic formula, himself, and then shot them both through the heart.

General Custer's chief scout during the Indian war of 1867 was Will Comstock, one of the most remarkable of the many remarkable men who have filled the atmosphere of the frontier with stories of daring. Custer says of him: "No Indian knew the country more thoroughly than he; perfect in horsemanship; fearless in manner; a splendid hunter; and a gentleman by instinct, as modest and unassuming as he was brave, he was an interesting, as well as a valuable, companion."

From the sole of his slender foot to the locks of his raven hair, he was a perfect scout, and a sleuth-hound on an Indian trail. His complexion was very dark, and he was said to be the son of a Delaware squaw by a white trapper, but no one ever actually knew his ancestry, or where he came from. He was unpretending and seclusive, but his exploits would fill a volume. Always superstitious, by virtue of his mother's blood, there seemed to be a cloud hanging over his life which made him avoid the haunts of men and seek his own companionship. He never had a "partner," as most scouts do, and when he undertook his perilous missions, he always went alone.

He died a victim of the treachery of the Indians.

He had been dispatched by General Sheridan to an Indian village to invite the chiefs to a council, and some of them started to return with him. After they had ridden a few miles together, and he was thrown off his guard, an Indian behind him leveled his gun and shot Comstock through the back, killing him instantly. Some of the chiefs who were in the party, months afterward told the circumstances of his death, and explained that the treacherous deed was done, not with their consent or expectation, but by this Indian of his own motive, to revenge the death of his father, whom Comstock had killed.

A conspicuous figure upon the plains for many years after the war of the Rebellion was the notorious William Hickok, or, as he was more generally known, "Wild Bill." This individual was at one time not only a famous, but a worthy, character, as worthy as men of his class often are, but dissipation and gambling turned a skillful guide and a brave scout into a worthless desperado. As Ned Buntline, the prolific writer of border romance, discovered "Buffalo Bill," Col. George Ward Nichols, the gallant soldier, and now the esthetic manager of the Cincinnati College of Music, and its annual Musical Festivals, discovered "Wild Bill." During the war Col. Nichols was in Missouri, in the army, attached to the headquarters of the commanding officer, and there he first became acquainted with the hero of so many bloody episodes, who was then a very brave, intelligent and valuable Union scout, more dreaded and feared by the rebels than any forty men in the Union Army. Indeed, most of the early homicides on Bill's long catalogue were the result of attempts to entrap or betray him by the rebel sympathizers of Missouri.

Hickok went into the army as a private in an Illinois regiment, and his home was in one of the small towns in the interior of the state. His regiment was sent to Missouri, where his remarkable nerve, his desperate recklessness and general intelligence, soon attracted the attention of the commanding officer, who made use of him as a scout. He was afterward detailed from his company and attached to the headquarters of General Curtis in that capacity. His services are highly commended by his commander, and he performed such feats of daring, and had such wonderful escapes as to make him the text of a great many interesting chapters of both history and romance. Col. Nichols introduced him to the public in a sketch published in a widely circulated magazine near the close of the war, and it gave the scout great fame.

Bill was a remarkable man in appearance as well as in experience. He was six feet two inches tall, slender, and as straight as an arrow. His face was small for so large a man, his profile regular, and he habitually wore a pleasant expression. Until the close of the war, when he went on the plains, he did not wear long hair, nor beaded buckskin garments, nor did he drink liquor or gamble,—those accomplishments he acquired after he became famous.

After "Wild Bill" went to Kansas, he fell into bad ways. He kept a saloon and a gambling house, and killed many men, both on his private account and officially, as the sheriff of the town of Abilene. During General Hancock's campaign in 1867, he was the chief of scouts, and General Custer, in his description of the events of that summer, says of him:

"Whether on foot or horseback, he was the one of the most perfect types of manhood I ever saw. His influence among frontiersmen was unbounded, and his word was law. Wild Bill is anything but a quarrelsome man, yet no one but himself can enumerate the many conflicts in which he has been engaged, and which have invariably resulted in the death of his adversary. I have personal knowledge of a dozen men he has killed, one of them being a member of my own command. Others have been severely wounded, but he always escaped unhurt. Yet in all the affairs of this kind in which Wild Bill has performed a part, there is not a single instance, in my knowledge, in which the verdict of twelve fair-minded men would not have been pronounced in his favor. That the even tenor of his way continues to be disturbed by little events of this character may be inferred from an item in the press, which states that 'the funeral of Jim Bludso, who was killed the other day by Wild Bill, took place to-day.' It then adds, 'the funeral expenses were borne by Wild Bill.' What could be more thoughtful than this? Not only to send a fellow mortal out of the world, but to pay the expenses of his transit."

Wild Bill finally became a refugee from justice, and after "removing" numerous sheriffs, detectives and other officers of the law, was shot down like a dog, in Deadwood, several years ago, by a man whom he had tried to murder.

"Buffalo Bill," before he left the plains for the "dramatic arena," was also a frontier figure along the Santa Fe Trail, and was originally a protege of "Wild Bill," serving under him as Deputy Sheriff at Abilene.

CHAPTER V.

TO THE AZTEC NAZARETH.

The extinction of the buffalo had really more to do with securing the peace and the settlement of the plains than the soldiers. The army could and did whip the Indians, but they wouldn't stay whipped, and as long as there was game to be had upon the prairie there were bands of red-skins pursuing it. A hunting party was very easily changed into a war party, and to the unprotected settler the two meant the same, but soon after 1867 the buffalo began rapidly to disappear. They were slaughtered by hundreds of thousands for their robes and tongues, and when those two marketable commodities were removed the rest of the carcass was left for the wolves. The whole prairie from the Missouri River to the Rocky Mountains, and from the northern boundary to the Rio Grande, is one vast sepulchre with the unburied bones of the bison lying in all stages of decay upon the ground. Thousands of men made a business of killing buffalo, and it was a profitable one. Two hundred thousand skins have been purchased at Omaha in a single year, and Bismark and Leavenworth, Cheyenne and Denver were also great markets.

Deprived of the sustenance nature provided for him, the Indian was compelled to remain at his agency

A SUMMER SCAMPER.

for food, and the settlers on the skirmish line of civilization were deprived of his disagreeable society. Occasionally mutinous bands have broken away from the agencies and swept over the state leaving a havoc of horrors behind them, but the country is so well populated now as to afford itself protection.

At one time during the early days of the Santa Fe Trail, the prairies were covered by vast droves of wild horses, known as mustangs, a cross between the Indian pony and the American horse. The name mustang is derived from a Mexican word signifying "no owner," and was originally used to designate stray steeds, but it became applied only to the wild horses which escaped from the Indians and roamed at large on the prairie, the toughest and least tractable animals that can be imagined.

At Florence, which is about 175 miles from Kansas City, the traveler enters what was the favorite hunting ground of the savage fifteen years ago, where are now some of the finest and most profitable cattle ranches in the world. The business of the ranchmen here is to take the rough cattle as they come from Texas and fatten them for the finest grades of beef.

Around Newton, where was a wild and desolate prairie ten years ago, is now a settlement of 15,000 Mennonites, Protestant refugees from Russia, a prosperous, thrifty people of Quakerish customs and appearance, who brought their silk worms with them from the old country, and are now cultivating cocoons with great success and profit. Kansas will some time be the great silk-growing district of this continent.

At Sterling is the center of the sorghum sugar

district, and on either side of the track can be seen large mills where the cane is ground and the juice boiled into syrup.

Fort Dodge is the headquarters of the cattle trade. It is the end of "the long drive," where the herds from the ranches of Texas, Indian Territory, New Mexico, and Western Kansas reach the cars, and is mostly populated by cowboys, drovers, gamblers and prostitutes. The ranchmen hold their assemblies there, and it is a sort of rendezvous, employment agency, pay station, and loafing place for the cowboys. If a ranchman wants a gang of herdsmen he goes to Dodge City, where hundreds are usually lying around awaiting an engagement. Those who are employed buy their "outfits" there—their ponies and saddles and blankets, and the supplies of bacon, flour, coffee, and canned goods for the camp commissary. After the "round up" in the spring, the cows and calves and bulls are turned loose upon the plains, and the steers are driven to Dodge City, where the owner receives his money from the Chicago or Kansas City buyer, and the cowboy is paid off for his winter's work. Then pandemonium reigns. The reckless youth who has been lying idle on the plains all winter, sleeping in a shaack or tent and watching the herds, takes a vacation, the length of which is determined by his supply of funds, and he generally manages to make Rome, or, rather, Dodge City, "howl."

As the cowboy population is migratory, the permanent residents of the place are the saloon-keepers, the gamblers, and the occupants of dens of vice who live on the spring harvest. They control the town and its government, a community of harpies, human vultures, preying upon the weaknesses and the vices of reckless men. A distinction should always be drawn between a "tough" and a "rough" in the language of the frontier. A "tough" is a reckless man, but not a vicious one. He will fight and shoot, but he will not steal. He has a kind heart, and generally, when sober, a good-natured and accommodating disposition. He is immoral, but not criminal. A "rough" is the reverse. He lives to plunder and plunders to live, and the cowboy is his victim. Nearly every spring there is a grand row at Dodge City between the cowboys and the roughs, and in the parlance of the former class, it sometimes becomes necessary for them to "take the town." They will spend their money recklessly in all forms of debauchery and dissipation, and the gambler, with his worse associates, will gather it all in; but when it comes to actual robbery, the cowboys resist and have their revenges. In the spring of 1882, they murdered the Chief of Police. As one of them related the circumstances to the writer, this official, a gambler, was in the habit of locking up "tenderfeet"—that is, newcomers—and, after robbing them of their money, notify them to leave town. This was all right as long as the operation was confined to tenderfeet, but it was tried on a cowboy who had been East for a visit and came back wearing "a short-horn collar and a bald-faced shirt." By these signs he was supposed to be a greenhorn, and the plan of official robbery was tried on him. He resisted, and the cowboys came to his aid. The Chief of Police was "plugged," as the narrator expressed it, and the cowboys "took the town."

One who is not familiar with the frontier can not realize the fury of these feuds and the absolute recklessness of those who participate in them. Human life is not held in even as great value as the cattle that are driven to market. The man who steals a steer dies; he who murders a fellow creature goes unpunished and unrestrained.

At Garden City the traveler reaches the end of the natural agricultural area, and enters a latitude where the rain-fall is never sufficient to sustain the crops. From this point west, all agriculture is carried on by means of irrigation, which is the most successful method of farming in the world; the absolute certainty of crops and the increased yield more than justifying the expense. The natural slope of the country is so great as to make it easy to obtain plenty of water from the mountain streams, which is conducted in canals or *acequias*, as the Mexicans call them, through the valleys. Each farmer and gardener has his private ditch connecting with the main channel, and at stated intervals flood his soil by opening the dam. The main canals are generally constructed and owned by stock companies, to whom the farmer pays so much per cultivated acre each year, as the householder in cities pays his water tax. Irrigation is older than history. The Egyptians used the system in the time of Moses, and the Pueblo Indians were using it when Coronado found them in his great march of 1540. How and where they got the idea is a favorite topic for the discussion of ethnologists, many of whom believe them to be the connecting link between the scattering of the nations at the time of the Tower of Babel and the pre-historic settlement of the American continent.

There is something curious in the undisputed fact that the rainfall of a country increases with its settlement. There are heavier, more frequent, and more regular showers in Kansas and New Mexico, and, in fact, in all the Western States and Territory, than there were twenty, or even ten years ago, and the records of the meteorologists show a gradual but consistent advancement of the boundaries of the arable area of the prairies according to its settlement. In 1845 vegetables could not be grown at Topeka, in 1870 they could not be grown at Newton, in 1872 they could not be grown at Larnard, and in 1879 attempts at gardening at Dodge City were pronounced failures, but at all these places now, as large and prolific crops can be produced as anywhere in Ohio or Illinois. The accepted theory of this remarkable climatic change is that the turning of the sod tends to increase the moisture of the atmosphere, which in its turn produces clouds and rain. The soil is sandy, and absorbs the rainfall so rapidly that the turf does not retain it long enough to permit of its evaporation, and when it has once soaked through, the sod acts as a shelter from the sun and wind. Ploughing deprives the earthen reservoir of its protection, and the sun sucks the moisture back into the air. But all theories aside, the fact stands that rain follows agricultural progress, and is limited or abundant according to the extent of the cultivated area.

Beyond Garden City, the railroad enters the great cattle ranges of the West, which extend to the Rocky Mountains in one direction, to the British boundary in another, and to the Rio Grande River southward. The raising of cattle is becoming a gigantic monopoly, and is no longer free to any who wish to enter it. Large companies, with enormous capital, have absorbed the property of the individual ranchmen, either by purchase or by the less honorable method of "freezing out." Whoever owns the land along the streams and around the springs, commands the free grazing area upon the hills and plateaus, and the water rights are rapidly coming into the possession of corporations, who permit no trespassing upon their property. Thus the owners of small herds, which for years roamed upon the government land without asking leave of any one, are finding themselves cut off from water supplies, and are obliged to sell to the monopolists. The Colorado Cattle Company, the Prairie Cattle Company, and other large corporations monopolize almost the entire area of Colorado, Western Kansas, New Mexico and Texas, and it is only a matter of time when they will secure every river and brook, and thus control the trade. A vast amount of foreign capital is invested in the stock of these corporations.

At La Junta (pronounced La Hoonta) the railroad splits, one branch running to Pueblo and connecting with the several lines of the Denver and Rio Grande for the mining regions of Colorado and Utah, and the other crosses the border into New Mexico.

From La Junta to the New Mexican line stretches

a sandy desert, watered only by the Purgatoire (or, as the natives pronounce it, the "Picketwire") River, but once across the boundary, the road enters a vast fertile tract, known as the Maxwell Grant.

About fifty years ago two Canadian Frenchmen, Beaubien and Miranda, who were traders at the old Indian Pueblo of Toas, procured from the Spanish government, through the influence of Governor Armijo, of New Mexico, the grant of an enormous tract of land, lying in the Northwest corner of the territory, and embracing 2,000,000 acres. Just what consideration the Spanish authorities received for this concession has never been satisfactorily explained, although the story goes that Beaubien and Miranda agreed to settle it with emigrants from Canada, and it is supposed that Governor Armijo, who was never above making an honest penny, received a handsome compensation for his services. It is the finest grazing ground on the continent, and its water privileges are almost priceless.

The daughter of Beaubien was married to an old scout and hunter named Lucien B. Maxwell, who was the chum and partner of Kit Carson. Hunters, and scouts, and miners always travel in couples; they did so fifty years ago, as they do to-day, and Kit Carson and Maxwell were "pards." Together they hunted and trapped for the Hudson Bay Company, and sold their skins at St. Vrains Fort, near where Denver now stands; together they fought the Indians and rescued beleaguered travelers upon the plains; together they piloted Fremont across the continent, and the Pathfinder's "Narrative" is a tribute to their skill as guides and scouts.

Maxwell inherited, through his wife, Beaubien's share of the grant, and built him a fine place at the Cimarron River, herding large numbers of cattle and sheep, and prospecting for silver and gold in the Raton (pronounced Rattoon) Mountains. Maxwell was a "free-handed" man, good natured and generous, and his ranche was the rendezvous for a large number of cronies, who assisted him in having a good time and spending his money. Finally he became embarrassed and sold his grant for $1,000,000 to a company of British capitalists, who in turn, sold it to a party of bankers at Amsterdam, Holland. They sent an agent over to look at their purchase, who discovered that land was covered with squatters, whom it would require years of litigation and an immense sum of money to remove. A young man named Frank Sherwin was selected as agent and manager, and he organized a corporation known as the Maxwell Grant Company, the Holland capitalists taking a great part of the stock in exchange for a deed to the property, and the rest was sold in New York and Chicago, to raise money for the development of the land and the removal of the squatters. Cyrus H. McCormick, George M. Pullman, N. K. Fairbank, Marshall Field, and other well-known capitalists of Chicago became interested, and still own a good portion of the stock.

Sherwin was manager, and erected a magnificent castle near the town of Springer, which was furnished and equipped in a luxurious manner. Decorators and upholsterers, plumbers and cabinet-makers, were sent from Chicago at a cost of many thousands of dollars, to prepare a palace fit for a king. The carpets and curtains were imported from Paris, and the cellar was filled with the rarest wines. A library was purchased in Chicago, and the most costly silverware and ornaments were selected at Tiffany's in New York. Here Sherwin still lives in the most princely style as the manager of one of the finest cattle ranches in the world.

There are several other magnificent residences owned by cattle kings in the same locality, one of them having been erected, and at one time occupied, by ex-Senator Dorsey, of Arkansas, who was compelled to sell it to James W. Bosler, a banker of Carlisle, Penn., in order to meet the expenses of his defence in the Star Route trials.

A few miles below Springer is a place called Wagon Mound, and near it are two flat-topped hills. This was the scene of a massacre many years ago. The Indians attacked a train of traders and emigrants, murdered all the people, stole the stock, and piled the wagons in a great heap upon one of the hills.

Further down is a high, sharp peak, which rises several hundred feet into the air, and can be seen for many miles. In 1837, there was a war between the Indians and the Mexicans, and the former invited their enemies to a great council and feast at the top of this peak, it being mutually agreed that all weapons should be discarded in the camp below. While this feast was in progress, the Indians slipped away one by one, ran down the side of the hill, got their arms, raided and destroyed the Mexican camp, and then surrounded the peak upon which were their defenceless enemies. To descend was certain death; to remain was starvation, but the Mexicans preferred the latter, and their bones lay unburied on the crest of the hill for many years. The scene of this horrible treachery is called Starvation Peak.

A few miles from Los Vegas are the famous Hot Springs, a favorite resort for tourists and invalids, and the mineral waters have achieved some remarkable cures. A magnificent hotel, called "The Montezuma," has been erected here, and furnishes a delightful place for the traveller to pass a few days of rest in the journey across the continent.

Twenty-five miles down the road is a sacred spot, the Nazareth of the Aztecs, the old pueblo of Pecos, where Montezuma was born. It matters not that the records of the church and the state, the official documents at the capital of Mexico, and the truth of history flatly contradict the romantic legend in which the dirty inhabitants of the New Mexican pueblos devoutly believe, the story remains one of the most charming that can be found in the folk-lore of our land.

These people are remarkable for many things, but for nothing more than their sincere and abiding faith in the sacred truth of the stories of their Redeemer's birth. According to their traditions Montezuma was born at Pecos, and the circumstances of his birth and youthhood are strangely similar to those that we read in the New Testament of the days of the Child Christ. When he grew to manhood he became their prophet, priest, and king, and a few miles south of the pueblo, near the cluster of shanties that surround a railroad tank, and is known by the Israelitish name of Levy, he built a church, at which, according to their traditions, the Aztec religion was born. They are not true, but are nevertheless charmingly interesting. The Aztecs worshiped fire, and Montezuma's principal business, when he grew to manhood, was to keep the flames upon the hideous old altar alive.

One day a great white eagle came and bore Montezuma away on his back. Everywhere the eagle alighted on the journey southward a pueblo arose, and the end of the flight was at the base of Popocatapetl, where the City of Mexico was founded by Montezuma, and a long line of kings of his name reigned for centuries at the great seat of the Aztec faith and power. Then Cortez came with his gallions, captured the city of the Montezumas, murdered the king, stole his gold, and sent the treasure across the water to the halls of the Alhambra.

Before Montezuma left Pecos, so they say, he told them he would come back as he went, and through the long centuries when they suffered the most cruel peonage that ever enslaved a people from their Spanish conquerors, the devout and confiding Aztec would go to his house-top at sunrise, and, shading his eyes with his dusky hand, would scan the far horizon of the south in the hope that his Messiah would appear; and he does it to this day, not only at Pecos but at all the pueblos which remain as relics of the Aztec days.

When Montezuma soared away he told his people that they must keep the fire on the altar burning until he reappeared, and at the old church, whose walls he laid of adobe, six feet thick, this injunction was obeyed until the travel became so frequent along the Santa Fe Trail that the priests feared the vandals would extinguish it, and prevent the coming of their Redeemer; so they took it one day with great ceremony over the mountains to the Pueblo of Taos, where, according to tradition, Montezuma's eagle first alighted in its flight from Pecos. There it is supposed to burn to-day in a secluded *estufa*, or temple, piously guarded from the sight or touch of the unbelievers, and safe from the sacrilegious hand of the cowboy whom the Pueblos fear as much as they reverence their mythical Messiah.

The old town of Pecos was no doubt a fortified pueblo of the Aztecs, and stands to-day, as it has stood for many centuries, built upon a great rock, which bears the shape of the human foot. It was founded no one knows when, as there are no records, and tradition is a lie. It can be seen at the left of the track, and farther down on the right, a thousand feet from the car windows, is a heap of adobe ruins which mark the spot where stood Montezuma's church. It can be plainly seen, but has been stripped by the hands of vandals of everything except its sacred memories.

It would be difficult to imagine a more picturesque valley than that which bears the Pecos River in its bosom. It is not only beautiful, but the soil is rich, the grass is superb, and there is plenty of water for cattle and irrigation purposes; the mountains are full of precious metals, and there are inexhaustible mines which need only capital and energy to develop them. In the control of men less indolent than the Mexicans, this valley would have been an Eden hundreds of years ago, but it stands to-day for a great part as it was when it left the hand of the creator, awaiting Yankee enterprise to develop its richness. A few miles below the old Pecos church is the famous Glorietta Pass, through which the railroad trains follow the old Santa Fe Trail. The pass is full of ranches, and those who occupy them have grown rich from their herds.

The narrowest portion of the pass is known as the Apache Canon, a cleft between the great rocks just wide enough to permit a dashing creek and a railroad train to pass. This, like most other portions of northeastern New Mexico, is historical. It was here that the greatest battle of the war, west of the Missouri River, was fought.

In 1863 the Confederates, and particularly the Texans, concluded that it would be a good idea to split the continent and capture the Territories. They had assurances of Mormon aid, and Duke Gwin promised that California would shake herself out of the folds of the flag if guaranteed co-operation from the South. It was a fair prospect and a tempting opportunity. There were few soldiers in New Mexico or the other Territories, and, once occupied by the Confederate forces, it would require an enormous army to recover the possession of the Rocky Mountain region and the great Pacific slope. The work was assigned to General Sibley, of the Confederate army, who was familiar with the country, and he marched at the head of an invading army of 10,000 Texans. Santa Fe, Albuquerque, and other Mexican towns yielded without a struggle, and welcomed the rangers with open arms. At the former place was Fort Marcy, an arsenal, which furnished arms and ammunition to the invaders, permitting the equipment of 2,000 Mexican soldiers and Indians, who filled the gaps left by the garrisons that were left at several points along the road.

The Union men of the frontier were alarmed, and dispatched couriers to the East with the news of Sibley's advance and petitions for military aid. But the situation was as critical in Virginia as it was in the West, and the entire attention of the administration was directed to the weakened and disheartened armies of the Potomac. Despairing of government aid, the patriots of Colorado and New Mexico determined to organize resistance on their own account. A regiment was organized at Denver, composed of hardy frontiersmen.

While Sibley and his troops were drinking the native wines of Bernalillo, the Colorado patriots, with no equipments but their own rifles and blankets, no commissions but their own patriotism, and no reward but the consciousness of loyalty, came down the foothills of the Rocky Mountains and spread their blankets in Glorietta Pass. The odds were ten to one, but when the clash came, in the Apache Canon, the dead Texans were piled up in heaps for three miles, and the live ones fled across the country into their own State. Santa Fe and the rest of the Territory was recaptured, and the great West was saved to the Union.

CHAPTER VI.

THE PEAKS AND CANONS OF COLORADO.

AFTER the grand march of Coronado, and the conquest and occupation of New Mexico, three hundred years ago, the Spaniards penetrated far into Colorado and Utah, exploring the country and prospecting for silver and gold, but were either exterminated or driven out by the savage Indians of the mountains, who were not as easily conquered as the peaceable Pueblos farther south. But the first reliable knowledge the world received of Colorado was from the report of Lieut. Pike, whose adventures are given in a previous chapter. He occupied a camp for some time near where the city of Pueblo now stands, and from it made explorations in different directions, at one time attempting to ascend Pike's Peak, but was overtaken by a snow storm and nearly perished. He penetrated far into the mountains, and after the most frightful sufferings and the loss of half his command, turned up in New Mexico, a prisoner of war. In 1832 trading posts were established along the foot of the mountains, and frequently lumps of gold which had been picked up in the streams and gulches were brought in by the Indians. In 1857 gold was found by a Georgia miner named Green Russell, in Cherry Creek, near where Denver stands, and when the news reached the border States, there was intense excitement. Several hundred men spent the winter of 1858 at Denver, and the town was then started. By the spring of 1859 the excitement was at fever heat, and long trains of wagons continued to move across the prairies, until the Kansas Pacific Railroad was opened twelve years later.

The town of Pueblo was originally a Mexican settlement around the ranch established there some time in the thirties. General Fremont found it in his first expedition of 1842, and made it a rendezvous for his men. It was called *the* Pueblo, and the name has clung to it. For the last twenty-five years it has been a prominent out-fitting post for miners, and during the Pike's Peak excitement, was a commercial centre of some importance, but Denver entirely overshadowed it, and not until the railroad was finished did Pueblo take on the appearance of a city. It is now the third town in Colorado, and takes pride in the expectation of becoming the Pittsburg of the State. It has several important manufactories, including the finest steel works outside of Chicago, in the country.

The State of Colorado owes much of its past, present and future prosperity to one man, General William J. Palmer, the President of the Denver & Rio Grande Railroad, who, with his associates, has made the development of its enormous resources possible. It was he who pushed a narrow-gauge track through all these valleys, over the tops of mountains which Fremont was unable to cross, and into canons where even the sure-footed mule could not go. Never was there such an exhibition of business audacity or engineering skill. The road was built upon a foundation of faith, but it will be fully justified. No longer the prospector coerces his dreary burro over the desolate plains and into the dismal wilderness; no longer the patient oxen propel the prairie schooner laden down with a scanty supply of actual necessities. To-day the miner rides to the mouth of his prospect hole in a Pullman palace car, and the farmer ships his cattle, his farming implements, and his household goods to the very land which the government gives him for the notary's fees.

It was in 1870 that the Denver & Rio Grande Railroad was begun, a few weeks after the Kansas Pacific crossed the plains and gave Denver a connection with the Missouri River. The original intention was to run a grand trunk line of road down the eastern base of the Rocky Mountains to Mexico, and pierce the mountains by branches to such mining districts as should prove sufficiently productive, but, as the branches became more important than the main line, the original plans were abandoned, and the Mexican territory was left for other enterprises to capture. From the date the first rail was laid the construction has been almost uninterrupted, but in the efforts to reach the storehouses where nature has hidden her treasures the greatest engineering difficulties that ever confronted a track-layer on either continent were encountered and overcome. Five times does the road cross the great continental divide, the backbone of America, and the summits are reached and left with grades that have no parallel in any part of the world. At one place on the road—the Crested Butte

Branch—the grade is 410 feet to the mile, almost incredible, but true, and at many places, it is between two and three hundred. In August, 1881, the Gunnison extension was opened, and the engineers began to push forward toward Utah. . This branch, which has recently been completed, is the longest and most valuable to the company, and for many reasons the most important to the public of any recently constructed railroad, opening as it does a hitherto inaccessible portion of the country that is of exhaustless wealth, and furnishing another through line across the continent.

At Pueblo the Denver & Rio Grande Railroad branches off in several directions. By taking the southern line, the traveler can reach Santa Fe, or the silver regions of San Juan, crossing the wonderful Veta Pass. By the western line he can go to Leadville, Gunnison, Salt Lake City or San Francisco, and northward, four or five hours' ride, is Denver, the route thither passing the foot of Pike's Peak. If he be a tourist, he should spend a few days in Denver visiting the great Mining Exposition, and should then go to Colorado Springs and Manitou, the Saratoga of the west, climb to the top of Pike's Peak to visit the lonely signal service observer, and view some of the grandest scenery in the world.

Bayard Taylor—a traveler who had seen almost everything of interest upon the earth's surface, from the geysers of Iceland to the cascades of the Amazon, and who studied it all with the soul of a poet, and the eye of an artist—once said that the grandest cluster of mountains in America, those offering the

A SUMMER SCAMPER.

most variety of outline and the most impressive stature, was that of which Pike's Peak is the centre, as they are approached from the plains east of Colorado Springs. I do not believe Mr. Taylor ever saw the Uncompahgre peaks, that loom up a white silhouette against a blue sky, south of Gunnison; but permitting his judgment to stand unquestioned, the traveler will see between Pike's Peak and the Soldier's Summit of the Wasatch Range, from the windows of the cars, mountains whose solemn and superlative grandeur paralyze the pen.

In no other part of the world can such a wilderness of mighty peaks be seen as along the 700 miles from Denver to Salt Lake City. Within the single distance of 100 miles there are sixty peaks over 13,000 feet high, or 7,000 feet higher than Mount Washington; a dozen that are over 14,000 feet high, and over 200 that are 5,000 feet higher than Mount Washington. The railroad track itself passes over summits that are nearly as high as the top of Mont Blanc, and there are several towns along its line that are much nearer the sky than the famous hospices of St. Bernard in the Alps.

The highest peaks on the Pacific coast are, Mount Shasta, California, 14,390 feet; Mount Hood, Oregon, 9,450 feet; Mount St. Helena, Washington Territory, 12,000 feet; Mount Adams, Washington Territory, 9,570 feet; Mount Baker, Washington Territory 10,700 feet; Mount Rainier, 12,360 feet; Mount Fairweather, Alaska, 14,708 feet; Mount St. Elias, Alaska, 16,750 feet; Mount Gleman, 12,000 feet.

The altitudes of Colorado range from 3,000 feet, the lowest, to about 15,700 feet, the highest, making an average of about 7,000 feet. In the most famous mountain regions of Europe and Eastern America, vegetation stops at an elevation of 5,000 feet; and in the Alps, the line of eternal snow is not higher than 7,500 feet. But in Colorado, vegetation ceases only at an altitude of 11,000 feet, and perpetual snow does not begin short of 13,500 feet. Fruits and flowers grow at an elevation of 11,000 feet, and heavy timber is found at 12,000 feet. The altitudes of the most important points in Colorado may be learned from the following table:

	Feet.		Feet.
Long's Peak	14,050	Mt. Æolus	14,054
Pike's "	14,216	Mt. Arkansas	13,647
Lincoln "	14,123	Mt. Byers	12,778
Yale "	14,078	Mt. Kendall	13,380
Harvard "	14,270	Mt. Holy Cross	14,176
Gray's "	14,145	Mt. Powell	13,398
Spanish Peaks	11,000	Mt. Ouray	14,043
Fremont's Peak	13,570	Mt. Rito Alto	12,989
Browns's Peak	15,690	Mt. Princeton	14,196
Mount Hooker	15,700	Mt. Wilson	14,280
Shavano	14,239	Mt. Audubon	13,402
Uncompahgre Peak	14,235	Mt. Cameron	14,000
Ute Pass	11,200	Mt. Elbert	14,351
Manitou	6,357	Mt. Evans	14,330
Mount Massive	14,368	Mt. Flora	12,878
Canon City	5,200	Mt. Guyot	13,565
Colorado Springs	5,990	Mt. Harvard	14,375
Denver	5,240	Mt. Lincoln	14,296
Leadville	10,247	Mt. Rosalie	14,340
Ouray	7,640	Mt. Yale	14,187
Mt. Hamilton	13,800	Mt. Sneffels	14,158

And in these mountains what glories dwell! What crags and caverns, what mighty rocks, upon which is written in a language that the eye of science can read the wonderful story of creation. Pages upon which the hand of God has traced the record of His mighty work, lie open on every side, and architecture which genius cannot imitate spreads itself before the amazed and awe-stricken witness. It is not necessary to leave the cars to see these spectacles; the railroad engineers have followed the clefts in the rocks as the fugitives of Scripture used to do, and from the window of a palace car the panorama can all be witnessed.

One of the grandest canons in the world is the Royal Gorge of the Arkansas, through which the railroad passes from Canon City to Salida, and which is familiar to all who have visited Leadville. Here is a mighty chasm cleft from the top to the bottom of the mountains, first by some awful geological commotion, and then worn smooth by the waters of the Arkansas river, that pour through it like a torrent. Only a few yards wide; only wide enough for the furious waters to pass through, the railway engineers were compelled to blast out a shelf in the side of a mighty precipice which towered 2,000 and sometimes 3,000 feet almost perpendicularly above them, in order to find a roadway for their rails. Below is the surging, furious torrent; above the seamed and shaggy cliffs of quartz, reaching half a mile toward the sky. In one place it was impossible to blast even a shelf in the rocks, so a bridge was stretched across the chasm, hung upon braces of steel riveted into the stone, and over that the train dashes. The shadow is deep and impressive, and the echoes of the engine's whistle and the rumbling of the cars follow one another like the laughter of Titans at play.

And to think of it, next to the ore and bullion that is hauled through there to the East from Leadville, the largest cargoes of freight are empty beer bottles from the mines in that range of the Rockies, to which the pious old Spaniards gave the name of "The Mountains of the Blood of Christ."

Just south of Salida, at the base of the mountains, are the famous Poncha Springs, the waters of which are similar to those of the Hot Springs of Arkansas, and to those of the popular resort at Los Vegas, N. M. There are forty-seven large springs already developed, and the average temperature of the waters is 150 deg. Fahrenheit. The medicinal qualities have not yet been practically tested, but the analysis shows that they contain the same chemical properties of the Arkansas and Los Vegas waters, and are no doubt heated in the same cauldron down below. The ownership of the springs has passed into the hands of parties recently from the Hot Springs of Arkansas, who are building an hotel and bath-houses, that will soon be ready for guests.

At Salida the road splits, one branch going to Leadville and the other to Gunnison over the wonderful Marshall Pass. As we leave Salida the track takes a wide curve around the valley, so as to attack the mountain it has to cross upon the flank, and distance is sacrificed to grade. Then, passing Poncha, we enter a narrow valley and hear the engine remonstrating with its measured "puff-puff-puff." Articles upon the seats of the cars roll off; overcoats that droop from the ceiling hang at an angle, and the floor of the car has a marked incline. We are going up a steep hill, so steep that it requires the labored effort of two engines to haul our little train of four narrow gauge cars. It is not a sudden leap over a small elevation and then down again, as we have been accustomed to on the prairies, but a steady rise, mile after mile. This is "the great continental divide" we are crossing—the backbone of North America, which stretches from Alaska to the Cordilleras in Mexico, and separates the Atlantic from the Pacific slope. Now, all the streams beside us flow into the Gulf of Mexico; pretty soon they will flow into the Gulf of California through the Grand Canon of the Colorado, which is the Mississippi of the West.

To cross the great divide, the track rises five thousand feet in thirty-eight miles, and the general grade is 210 feet to the mile. If the track were laid straight up to the summit it would make an angle of forty-five degrees, but as that is an impossibility in engineering, the only alternative is to climb the side of the slope at a diagonal, as cows and goats do; and the track looks on paper like a great coil around the mountain, embracing it as the bracelets that are made to represent serpents entwine around a lady's wrist.

The wonders of modern engineering are nowhere shown as plainly as here. It is the great horse-shoe curve of the Pennsylvania Railroad duplicated forty times, with nearly three times the grade. That has a grade of eighty feet to the mile. This is generally 210 feet, and in some places 217 feet to the mile.

We are running now on one side of a narrow little valley, with a furious trout stream a hundred feet or so below us. Down in the gulf, on the other side of the valley, along the bed of the brook, is the track we just passed over, and on the same side two hundred feet above us, hanging like a thread upon the side of the steep hill, is the track which we are soon to reach. Up, up, up, we go; the engines puffing and fretting; the fireman heaving in coal; the engineer with one hand on the throttle and the other on the steam-brake looking with all his eyes at the track before him, ready at an instant's notice to stop the train. Is it safe? Perfectly. If an accident should occur the train could be stopped in a quarter of a second. If one of the cars should become detached it would stop instantly, because of the automatic brakes that would fasten the wheels as firmly as the track itself. Cars have broken their couplings, but have been stopped and repaired before the passengers suspected what was the matter.

At the center of the curve, we turn on a semi-circular bridge across the valley, down which we look five or six hundred feet at the little brook that runs through the grass, carrying the melted snow from the mountain tops to moisten the prairies of Colorado and Kansas. Pretty soon we can see four rings of the coil, the track we are on, and one below us on our side of the ravine; two on the other side, one above, and one below. The one above on the other side is covered with snow sheds, for we are fast reaching the region of eternal snows, and are getting above the timber, line on a lifeless crust of earth which bears no fruit or beauty and calls for no emotion but the sense of an awful elevation, and pity at the waste of so much sunshine upon a soil that never knew a useful plant or a lovely flower. Masses of snow lie here and there in the fissures of the mountains, with threads of water trickling into the stream below. The conductor tells us that in some places the snow lies sixty-four feet deep, and that now and then, after a "warm spell," it becomes undermined by melting, and falls in a great avalanche down the mountain side. This is the reason the track is covered with a shed of heavy planks, supported by strong and rugged rafters.

At the top of the Pass, under a great shed, the train stops at a station where a gang of men is kept who walk the track by day and night inspecting every rail and tie to see that there is no cause of accident, and to clear away the rocks and snow that sometimes roll down from the summits of the mountains. The wheels and couplings of the cars are closely examined, and a skillful man with sharp eyes tests the brakes, for we are going down the mountains over a grade that is as steep and as crooked as that which we have just climbed. One of the engines is uncoupled and starts ahead, an avant courier, to clear the track and make safety doubly sure. As we come out of the snowsheds the air is clear and frosty. We are nearly eleven thousand feet high; almost twice as high as Mount Washington, as near Heaven as we ever were, and as near as some of the passengers will ever get. The snow is six or eight inches deep upon the track —it snows here every cloudy day—and the pioneer engine is plowing patiently through, making a path for the train. The view is as grand as mountain scenery can be. Snowy peaks tower above us, and here and there rocky ledges, to which the snow cannot cling, jut out like silhouettes against the sky. The chains of mountains rise and fall like the billows of the sea—a hazy succession of black curves, with now and then a cluster of peaks covered with the whitest of white snow—a regiment of hoary headed giants, and above them all, grand and impressive in its imperial majesty among mountains, rises Ouray, with its rugged head.

The Rocky Mountains and the Alps are often compared, to the disadvantage of the latter, by accomplished travelers who have seen both. While the Alps are more abrupt and full of pinnacles, there is just as grand and remarkable scenery here, and more of it. Call this the Switzerland of America? Not much. Let us call Switzerland the Colorado of Europe.

Slowly and carefully we descend. The same sharp curves, and the same coils of track terraced upon the mountain side; sometimes four and often three terraces being in sight at the same time, until at last, with our faithful engine scout ahead of us, we go bounding through the fertile valley of the Tomichi, and the city of Gunnison is soon reached.

Following the Gunnison River through its wide beautiful valley for a few miles, the mountains seem to close in upon the track, and it enters one of the grandest gorges in the world, known as the Black Canon of the Gunnison. The chasm is not so deep as that through which the Arkansas river flows, but it is longer and more picturesque, and the scenery is more diversified. Here are beautiful cataracts on both

A SUMMER SCAMPER. 89

sides of the track—which are not found in the Royal Gorge—the water tumbling down the mountain crags into the Gunnison River, over precipices from 1,500 to 2,000 feet high. In one place is a dainty little cascade, like the bridal veil at Niagara Falls—a slender thread of water pouring over the rocks in fine spray, and falling into a little basin close by the track, which makes as beautiful a picture as can be seen anywhere.

And what a magnificent stream is the Gunnison! Its waters are clear and cold, and the dark shadows of the cliffs falling upon it give it a tint of beautiful green. Springing from a region white with eternal snows, like a thread of silver, it burrows through the walls of rock whose pinnacles rise 2,000 and 3,000 feet high on either side, and is roofed in by a narrow strip of unsullied blue sky—so narrow that one standing on one cliff can throw a stone across to the summit of the other. Now the river frets and spumes and throws its foam, splashing spray against the black rocks; again it giggles and gurgles in glee, laughs and roars at the triumph of having leaped over nature's barriers; then tumbles headlong over a mighty rock, and with placid dignity flows along beside the great mountains, taking a few moments' rest in its mad race to the sea.

For fifty miles we follow the narrow chasm, steeped in the purple of a perpetual twilight. The solemn walls stand up 3,000 feet both sides of us, frowning down upon the intruders into their cloistered solitude. For a mile or two they are almost perpendicular, gray with the antique lichens that countless summers have gathered upon their purple fronts; then they are massed in broken columns standing upon a common base. Here a solitary pinnacle soars upward toward the sky like a monstrous cathedral tower; there the rocks have been thrown together helter-skelter in piles half a mile high by some remote geological commotion, and again they close together and hug the current of the river for unbroken miles, the shadows becoming darker and gloomier. In places the ledges are hacked and torn, seared and split into great seams into which earth has fallen, and there a few solitary spruce trees cling in a perilous existence. Often at a height which the sun's rays can sometimes reach, but the wind is never still, a tiny flower may be seen smiling with heroic fortitude, and a few feet away in a cleft in the rocks will be found an eagle's nest. When night approaches, the edges of the rocks that, standing out against the sky can catch the moonbeams, will be fringed with a silvery phosphorescence. Looking up, one sees the narrow roof of sky, with a fresco of stars; looking down, there is the blackness of darkness immeasurable.

Whose hand framed this great work? Who split these great mountains asunder, and when was it done? One might as well ask the age of a star. All we know is what the geologists read upon the rocks where God has written the record of his handiwork through the long cycles of creation. An awe inspires one when he thinks that all this architectural grandeur, all these mighty chasms which would have required 1,000,000 men 1,000 years to have excavated, have been wrought by the simple agencies of water and wind and dust! These canons were not made by volcanic eruptions, the geologists tell us, but by agencies so simple as those. They are all the channels of living rivers, and were carved out by the incessant waters. Hundreds of thousands of square miles of solid granite in these mountains have slowly yielded to the patient, but resistless, force of the stream and its invisible allies in the air, have crumbled into dust, and have been carried to the sea. These solemn walls had been standing for countless centuries in a silence broken only by the dash of the waters, until the railroad contractors brought their dynamite and blasted a passage through.

There was no natural roadway; not even a footpath, and no room for one. The river filled the entire bottom of the chasm, and every foot of the track is laid upon an artificial shelf blasted in the side of the precipice. It was a question of crossing the tops of the mountains or going through the gorge, and the latter alternative was chosen. In the winter of 1881-2 the surveyors went through on the ice, and the track-builders followed them. The river always freezes over, and upon its surface a foothold was found to do the work. J. R. De Remer was the engineer in charge, and, with his men, he slept in the holes of the rocks. It was necessary to hurry the work through, before the ice melted, and 3,000 men were engaged here at one time grading a roadway. Almost every foot of it was secured by blasting, and the cost averaged $150,000 a mile. The river falls rapidly and the grade is about 100 feet to the mile.

The traveler will notice that after riding through

the main canon for about thirty miles the road turns a sudden corner, crosses a bridge, enters a side canon, through which flows the Cimmaron Creek, and climbs a steep hill into the world again. It was found when this point was reached that it was not practicable to follow the canon any farther. The plan of blasting a roadway along the side of the precipice might have been continued, but the fall of the river was so rapid that the grade must necessarily have been from two to three hundred feet to the mile, and that, as all railroad men know, is impracticable for any distance. If the regular grade of ninety or one hundred feet to the mile that prevails in the other portion of the canon had been kept up, the track would have been a thousand feet higher than the water at the point where the river leaves the mountains and enters the valley.

It became necessary, therefore, to leave the main canon, and darting into a smaller one to follow it to the top of the hills, from which an easy descent is made by wide curves into the famous Uncompaghre Valley, from which the Ute Indians were removed only a year or so ago. Following the Uncompaghre River, the railroad train passes fine farms that were entered and broken in 1882, and produced magnificent crops which were readily sold at enormous prices in the mining camps.

The first town west of Montrose is called Colorow, after the famous Ute Chief, whose body now hangs, Indian fashion, suspended by ropes from the ceiling of a little cabin on the river bank, near by. The second town is Delta, where the Gunnison River is again encountered, and the road follows its circuitous wanderings again through another canon, not so wild, and grand, and impressive, but quite as picturesque, and affording even more interest to the scientist, because of its wonderful geological formations, and the fact that it is the sarcophagus of birds, and fish and insects, that were buried there millions of years ago. The formation is blood-red sandstone, and is so water worn, and in such an advanced state of decay, as to crumble almost with the force of the wind, revealing treasures that make the fossil hunter fairly dance with delight.

The deformities of nature are always picturesque and absurd, and it is almost impossible to conceive of a greater variety of grotesqueness than is presented in the appearance of these rocks. The tops of nearly all the hills are capped with piles of red sandstone, regularly laid like the battlements of a mediæval fortress in some places, and in others eroded into a resemblance of the turrets of a Normandy castle. Then come a series of clay cliffs, with the same sort of summits, which have been carved by the wind and rain and dust into forms as grotesque as if a goblin had been the architect, and presenting shapes in which an ingenious eye can trace the likeness of every bird and beast and reptile. It is a geological masquerade.

After leaving Grand Junction the railroad enters a veritable desert; a low, treeless, waterless and neglected waste. It is a sort of dry sea, in which the billows of sand rise and fall and shift hither and thither under the force of the wind. Yet the ride is not devoid of interest, for there is a fascination in a landscape so unfamiliar and unique. The grand range of the Sierra LaSalle Mountains looms up in the distance, broken into countless snow-covered peaks, whose unexplored canons are supposed to contain great deposits of treasure, which will soon be rooted out by prospectors. Near Thomson's Springs, a little station, the Indians have drawn rude hieroglyphics on the soft walls of the canon that interest and puzzle the archæologist.

At the crossing of Green River, the road runs parallel with an old trail said to have been made by the Spanish explorers, who came into Utah in the sixteenth century. The canons of the Green River are very grand, but are practically unexplored. North of the point where the railroad crosses, is a line of curious hills known as the Azure Cliffs from the curious color of the clay of which they are formed, and still further north is Desolation Canon, a wonderful geological structure which offers a tempting field for the explorer and the artist. A few miles to the south is the junction of the Green and Grand Rivers, which, coming together, form the Colorado, the largest and most sublime stream on the Pacific coast. It is a Niagara more than two thousand miles long. To the west, along the old Spanish trail, are the ruins of Indian villages hundreds of years old, supposed to have been destroyed by the Spanish explorers.

Soon Price River is reached, and later Castle Valley, at the entrance to which stand two great sandstone shafts, rising to a height of 500 feet, and looking like monstrous castles, with battlements and bastians, turrets and towers. They are just far enough apart to allow the railroad train to pass through, and present a grand and striking picture.

Through this narrow gate the train passes and climbs a steep grade, 200 feet to the mile, along a trail that was made by Albert Sydney Johnson, in 1861, when he led the troops of his command from Utah to join the Confederates in Texas. The scenery is wild and picturesque, constantly changing, and always beautiful. Crossing the great divide known as Soldiers' Summit, the road plunges into another great canon, from which it emerges into the beautiful Utah Valley, in the center of which lies a long, blue sheet of water known as Utah Lake. As far as the eye can reach are emerald meadows, blossoming orchards, and wheat fields of living green. The irrigation ditches cut the landscape like threads of silver, and thrifty Mormon villages, with their neat, white houses, and well-kept dooryards, break the landscape at frequent intervals. The valley is surrounded by grand mountain ranges, the Wahsatch on the east, and the Oquirrh on the west, whose bodies are covered with timber, and whose crests are crowned with everlasting snow. By the side of the lake stands the flourishing Mormon town of Provo, a popular watering place, and from it the railroad follows the famous river Jordan to Salt Lake City. The next town of size is Lehi, from which a branch road runs into the famous Cottonwood mining district, where the much discussed Emma Mine is located, on which the fortunes of statesmen have been wrecked.

Just before reaching Salt Lake City on the left side of the road is a cluster of houses and large barns, with a tiny school house in the center. This is the residence of George Q. Cannon, the leading man among the Mormons, and the future president of the church. He has a large farm, and a large family, four wives, who live in four pretty cottages, and any number of children, who are taught by a private tutor in a school house that the passenger can see.

From Salt Lake to Ogden the railroad track follows the shore of the great Salt Lake. On one side of the road the green waters stretch away to the distance, broken by massive mountains that rise from the islands in its bosom, and on the other side is the almost impassable Wahsatch range. Fertile and well kept farms follow in succession along the valley, under the shadows of the peaks, but beyond the lake, far to the west, is the Great American desert, that stretches from the Wahsatch Mountains to the Sierras of Nevada. It once held an inland ocean in its lap, of which the Great Salt Lake is the relic and residue.

CHAPTER VII.

THE CITY OF THE SAINTS.

The condition of the Mormon church has not changed much since the death of "Brother Brigham," as the Mormons call him. There was a little turmoil over the election of his successor as the President of the church, and at one time it was thought his two sons, John W. and Brigham, Jr., would make a row; but the latter was appeased by being chosen one of the twelve apostles, and John was sat down upon with emphasis. John never was a very pious man, and after being rejected by the church as a leader, he shook the dust of Zion from his indignant feet and went to New Mexico, where he secured a valuable railroad contract, and has since lived upon a ranch in Arizona. At the annual conference of the members of the Church of the Latter Day Saints, at Salt Lake City, in April, 1883, John appeared, made a penitential confession of waywardness, and renewed his allegiance to the church.

Two of Brigham's sons are in the United States army. One of them is said to be a brilliant fellow, and graduated from West Point at the head of his class. He is in the engineer corps, and is spoken of by officers as a thorough gentleman. Two of the daughters have gone to the bad. The Mormons admit it, but say they were led away by Gentiles. One of them, Emeline, is an actress on the variety stage, supposed to be in San Francisco, and the other, Dora, is said to be the mistress of a Salt Lake gambler

Eighteen of Brigham's widows live at Salt Lake City still. Ann Eliza (No. 19), the apostate, who took the lecture field, was married in May, 1883, to a merchant of Manistee, Mich. Some of the widows live with their families in the "Lion House" —so-called from the carved stones that cap the pillars of the entrances—where they lived during Brigham's lifetime, but the main building he occupied is now the headquarters of the church. None of the widows have remarried, reports to the contrary notwithstanding.

Amelia, it will be remembered, was the most attractive of Brigham's plurality, and was the recipient of his most conspicuous favor. She was too good to live in the prophet's harem, and he built for her, across the street from the Lion House, an elegant mansion of stone. It was furnished by him with costly luxuriance, and here he abode during the last years of his life in the bosom of his favorite, while across the way in the old adobe structure, which was erected soon after the exodus from Nauvoo, the other seventeen remained without a murmur. One would suppose that this marked favoritism would have raised a row around the prophet, but such was the family discipline that the other wives appeared only to admire Brigham's devotion to Amelia, and were glad to receive the merest smile from his beneficent face.

One can not but admire the matchless audacity and

ability of that man—the Apostle Paul of the New Dispensation. He had none of the disjointed, turbulent, and inconsistent fanaticism of Joseph Smith, but was cool and far-sighted, possessing unbounded physical and moral courage, an unpretentious authority that was felt in the smallest detail of the theocracy of which he was the head; with ability to plan and the energy to execute—a very Lion of the Lord, as the Saints used to call him—he was a combination of Napoleon, Robespierre, and Richelieu.

As long as Brigham lived, his authority was absolute; his utterances were received as revelations from on high, and although he was guilty in his public addresses of blasphemy and obscenity that would not have been tolerated from any other man, this people bowed before his will as the Hindoos bow before the wheels of Juggernaut. Amelia is said to have exercised a powerful influence over the prophet, and in a quiet way molded him to her will—the only being to whom he ever yielded; the Delilah of the Mormon Samson. The apostles and elders were more jealous of her than the other wives, and when the prophet died they got in their work. Her influence suddenly ended; her life of luxury suddenly ceased. She became as powerless and as friendless as the ex-Empress of France or the crazy Queen of Spain. It was discovered that "the Amelia palace," as her beautiful mansion was called, had been erected with the funds of the church, and she was unceremoniously ejected. With her share of the property Brigham left, she purchased a cozy little cottage in a retired portion of the town, and is living there in dignified and aristocratic seclusion. She retains much of her beauty, and is said to be a woman of strong intellect and commanding appearance. Courtiers came to woo her, and it was reported at one time that she had been "sealed" to one of the apostles, a business man who lives at Ogden, but she rejected his addresses, and still wears a widow's weeds. The Gentiles know little about her, but the Mormons say she is true to Brigham, and believes she will sit with him in glory. She was the wife of his old age and never had any children.

When Brigham was living, it was supposed that he was enormously wealthy, and he left a will bequeathing his property in equal shares among his eighteen wives and fifty or sixty children. But when the document went to probate, the church put in a claim for a large share of the estate, and it was found that the charge so frequently made was true, that Brigham had his own affairs so mixed up with his official responsibilities that he scarcely knew, if he cared, how much of it belonged to him and how much to Zion. The claims of the church were settled first, and the residue for the enormous family was much smaller than the heirs expected. It is not known exactly how much they got, as the local courts are controlled by the church, but it is generally supposed that the eighteen wives and the fifty children received about $30,000 apiece.

There was a good deal of dissatisfaction in some quarters at the distribution, and John W., as well as others of the heirs, at one time proposed to make a fuss about it; but the Gentiles say they were frightened out of the contest by the threats of the heads of the church, who offered to show that they were getting a good deal more than they were entitled to if the naked truth were known.

Brigham was the custodian of all the tithes—the pious Mormons pay into the treasury one-tenth of their incomes—and he never rendered an account to any one. After his death a demand was made of his successor to report a financial exhibit at the annual conference, and it was done for one or two years, but now it is submitted to the apostles, and not to the people.

A good many jokes have been made by the newspaper paragraphers about the army of widows watering the turf upon the prophet's grave with their tears, and it has been repeatedly stated in print that his burial place is neglected and unmarked. This is not true. His body lies on a terrace back of the Lion House, although it is not in the regular cemetery of the church. He died soon after the theft of A. T. Stewart's body, and the faithful people, fearing that some ghoul would steal his bones, buried them within the great wall he built to surround his harem and the offices of the church when Zion was frequently visited by hostile Indians. It is claimed by anti-Mormon writers that this wall, which encloses an area as large as three blocks of Chicago, was erected not so much as a protection from the Indians as a breastwork for resistance against the United States troops, but it would stand a poor show against a cannonade.

Careful precautions were taken to guard the body. A great flagstone, sixteen inches thick and weighing many tons, was placed at the bottom of the grave, and another like it was placed upon the coffin. The two were riveted together by rods of steel at narrow intervals, and when the horn blows on resurrection morning Brother Brigham will find himself in a tight place. Upon the top of the grave a marble slab is laid, which bears an appropriate inscription, and it is surrounded by a stalwart iron fence.

President John Taylor, the successor of Brigham Young, now occupies Amelia Palace with one of his wives—she who is said to be the original Mrs. Taylor. There are three more, but they do not dwell with him. Since the prosecutions for polygamy, those who have plural wives are very careful not to furnish evidence for the courts, and it is difficult to ascertain how many spouses a Mormon has, and who they are. The several families are scattered through the town, and each has a separate residence. It is a matter of common report that President Taylor's wives occupy certain houses, but it is impossible to determine the fact by legal testimony, so long as the wives themselves are permitted by law to refuse to testify.

A row of very pretty cottages are pointed out as the residences of the several Mrs. Sharp—the wives of one of the ablest and shrewdest apostles, who is the manager of that enormous institution known as Zion's Co-operative Store—but the ladies are known by their maiden names, and the children can offer no evidence of their parentage.

President Taylor is a venerable man, with a gentle eye, but a strong mouth, and a jaw that indicates courage and determination. He was with Joseph

Smith when the founder of Mormonism suffered "martyrdom" in the jail at Carthage, Ill., and to this day carries the marks of the assassins' bullets. He is getting old and feeble, and his mind is not so clear as it was; but he is the remnant of what was once a man powerful in mind and body.

The man whom the Mormons believe to be the infallible successor of the Savior of the world; the prophet who receives revelations from the Almighty, and the spiritual and temporal autocrat of Zion, can be found in a handsomely furnished library, surrounded by portraits of the leading men of the past and present, and visitors will be cordially received by him. The Gentiles say that Taylor is not so able as Brigham Young, but that he is a better man, and is respected and beloved where Brigham was feared. Taylor holds an elective office, and not a life position, as most people suppose. The head of the church, or, as his official title stands, "The Prophet, Seer, and Revelator, the President of the Church of Jesus Christ of Latter Day Saints all over the world," is elected every year at the spring conference, and, strange to say, there has never been any opposition to the re-election of Smith, Young and Taylor, the three men who have occupied the place for fifty-two years. At the time Brigham Young was elected after Smith was slain, there was a bitter contest which alienated some of the leading men, and resulted in a good deal of apostacy, but there was never any future opposition; and when Taylor was chosen after Brigham Young's death, there were several aspirants, but they are waiting till he dies, for under the

Mormon autocracy no one tries to step into a live man's shoes. George Q. Cannon will be the next President, by right of service, usefulness, and well-earned influence.

President Taylor has "revelations" occasionally, as Joe Smith did. He has them whenever the faith of the people needs strengthening, or the will of the President needs to be enforced. He had a revelation in the winter of 1882 that the Edmunds bill would not pass, and the deluded Mormons actually believe that it was true, and that the Almighty spoke to them through John Taylor, in the voice of prophecy, which was fulfilled. But Mr. Taylor does not go into the practice of revelations to any extent. The people are not so superstitious as they were, and cannot take revelations in such large doses as they wallowed in Joseph Smith's time and in the days of Brigham. There used to be a time when the church would listen to a revelation from the Lord through the lips of Brigham with as much awe as if the heavens had opened before their eyes, and the voice the Creator had spoken as it did to Moses. But the prophecy business was overdone. That resource was applied to oftener than was politic, for the words of the prophet did not always come true, and the people began to lose their faith. Joseph Smith prophesied at Nauvoo that the United States would be broken into fragments, and then the time of the fulfillment of the word which gives the Latter Day Saints the control of the world would come. When the announcement of the secession of the Southern States was read in the Tabernacle in 1861, the people thought the hour had surely arrived. This largely accounts for the sympathy of the Mormons with the South during the war.

I once asked a prominent Mormon about these "revelations;" how they came, and under what circumstances, and he said that they were very much misunderstood by "the world," as all that part of the universe outside of Zion is alluded to. He said there was never any pretension that a spirit from Heaven appeared to John Taylor or Brigham Young, nor did these revelations come in dreams; but when Mr. Taylor was troubled in his mind or undecided in an emergency, he sought the guidance of the Almighty in prayer, with faith, and the path of duty was revealed to him by a mental process, after prayerful reflection. When the Edmunds bill was pending in the Senate he prayed, and they all prayed, that it might not pass, and the confidence in its failure, which was inspired in Mr. Taylor's mind, was a "revelation."

Woman suffrage prevails here with a vengeance, and every Mormon woman votes as the president of the church, from the pulpit of the tabernacle, tells her to. Every ballot is numbered, and the number is set upon the registration books beside the name of her or him who casts it. Woe be to the Mormon who votes anything but the straight ticket. The woman suffragists have made a great ado lest the ballot be taken away from their sex in Utah, and, at the same time, they denounce polygamy as worse than slavery to the women who live in it. The slightest examination of the case will show them that the ballot in the hand of woman here is but one more link in the chain that binds her. Every vote cast by a female Mormon in Utah is a vote for the perpetuation of polygamy; and, strange as it may appear, the female portion of the Mormon Church is more loyal to its doctrines than the members of the other sex. Everybody in Salt Lake will admit that—Jew, Gentile, or Mormon. The most effective propagandists are women, and there is less apostacy among them than among the men. These are strange statements, but they are true.

Is polygamy increasing? There is no doubt of it. While it is impossible to get legal evidence of the fact, it is not denied by the Mormons, and is thoroughly believed by the Gentiles. The Mormons discuss the question freely, and defend the practice as ardently as a Baptist will defend the doctrine of immersion. While they will not say whether this man or that is a polygamist, and pretend ignorance as to when and by whom the transactions of the filthy "Endowment House" are engaged in, they claim that the practice is a sacred ordinance of the church, and that the more wives a man has the higher will be his place in glory. Detectives have been employed, it is said, to watch the Endowment House and spot those who enter it, but it is so protected by a great wall which surrounds the tabernacle and new temple, and its mysteries are conducted with such caution, that such schemes have long since been abandoned. At one time, when the prosecutions for polygamy were somewhat ardent, the people were frightened away from the place, but they have been spurred into it again by the leaders of the church, and the failure to convict has given them courage. It is the belief of the Gentiles now that within the last year or two plural marriages have been more numerous than ever before.

The system of serveillance which prevailed during the time of Brigham Young, by which he was enabled to know what was going on in the households of the people, the very words they spoke and the every act they did, is still kept up to a certain extent, although not so strictly, and it pertains to the spiritual condition almost entirely. There is no Brigham Young now, and his power has been distributed among many.

The bulwarks of Zion—of which we have all read, in the old geographies—are almost gone. There used to be a wall around the Holy City, six miles in length, twelve feet high, six feet broad at the bottom and three at the top, with embrasures, and bastions, and buttresses, and all that sort of thing, erected as a defense against the Lamanites, as the Indians used to be called in church lingo; but at one time it was believed, and perhaps intended, that this wall, like that around the prophet's house, was for the purpose of protecting the saints from the United States Government. Now they use the courts, and their bulwark is the ballot-box and the full coffers of the church.

The Danites, which have been the theme of so much controversy, and so much blood and thunder romance, are obsolete. There is no longer any use for them. The Gentiles are too numerous, and too well armed, and the power of the government is too strongly represented by its officials and ten companies of soldiers at Fort Douglas.

Bill Hickman, the notorious leader of the Danites in olden times, whose name was once a terror to emigrants from the Missouri River to the Pacific Ocean, is still alive, and lives in the eastern part of the Territory, a decayed horse-thief and murderer. He is said to occasionally indulge in a violation of the law nowadays, stealing a stray steer or a vagrant pony, but he no longer eats a Gentile for breakfast every morning, and is living upon his reputation as a cutthroat. Hickman still claims to be a Mormon, but the Mormons repudiate him, say he never belonged to the church, and claim that the murders he committed were done on his own account, and not under the doctrine of "blood atonement," of which so much has been said. He has written an autobiography, or hired some scribbler to write one for him, in which he gives the organization of the Danites, and a list of the crimes he claims to have committed under the orders of the church. The Gentiles have little faith in him or his stories, and agree with the Mormons that he is the greatest villain unhung.

It is generally supposed that the Gentile population is growing more rapidly than that of the Mormons, but it is not true. At one time, when there was a rush into the mines, it was the case, but it is so no longer, and now the Mormons are increasing very fast. In 1882, 3,500 immigrants were brought in by the Mormon missionaries, and the non-Mormon immigrants were probably not more than two-thirds of that number. The Gentile immigrants are mostly males, laborers who came to work in the mines, while the Mormon accessions are largely composed of women. Among the Gentile population the males are very much in excess, being four to one. Among the Mormon population the sexes are about even, so that marriages are frequent, families are large, and the increase from natural causes is five or six times as great as among the Gentiles. So that, instead of Mormonism dying out, it is flourishing like plants in a hot bed. The Mormon immigrants come mostly from Europe, from Denmark, Scandinavia, and England, the latter country furnishing the larger number. Of late years there have been very large accessions from the Southern States, and recently a colony of 300 came in from Tennessee; although 80 per cent. of the emigrants are foreigners. There are usually between three and four hundred Mormon missionaries in the field, in all parts of the world, and their success can not be wondered at when it is known that there is a large fund used constantly for paying the expenses of emigrants, and that it is liberally dispensed.

The missionaries are moving among the poorest; most ignorant classes in civilization, but to no place can they go where the knowledge of America's advantages for the poor has not gone before them. The inducement given in the payment of their passage to America is stronger than any religious delusion can be, and the Mormon doctrines and practices have very little influence comparatively among the classes who accept the advantages offered. When they arrive, the immigrants are taken to the Tithing House, and from there they are distributed over the Territory. The farmers are located on government lands, and the mechanics are sent to the various "stakes" of Zion, as the settlements are called. Every one is taken care of, and the poor are provided with all the necessaries of life, from the funds of the church, until they can provide for themselves. But every dollar that is expended for them is charged to the family that receives it, and the first money they earn is demanded and collected to reimburse the treasury. In this way the immigration fund is kept large and self-sustaining, and not a cent is ever expended that does not come back to the church with interest. A good many of the new-comers are sent into Idaho and Arizona, where there are large and growing Mormon settlements. It is no longer true that comely women are selected for the harems of the heads of the church. It may have been the fact once, and now and then there may be an instance where a missionary becomes enamored of one of his proselytes and "seals" her to himself upon their arrival at Zion, but even the Gentiles deny that the practice prevails to any extent.

Horrible stories are told about the condition of the Mormon immigrants when they arrive, and of their treatment on the way. They are the lowest, filthiest, most ignorant class of people, but they are subject to no more hardships, and their condition is no worse than the train loads of immigrants that can be seen going to Manitoba and other parts of the West. There is no doubt that they are treated like cattle, but they have been born and bred in conditions that are worse than American farm cattle live in, and a comparison of their hardships to-day with the hardships of those who came across the plains twenty-five years ago shows a marked improvement. Now they come on rapid railway trains; then they were compelled to follow a weary and death-haunted pilgrimage across the plains, a march that surpassed in dangers and hardships that of the Israelites, under the lead of Moses, from Egypt to the promised land. They crossed the mountains at a pass eighteen miles from Salt Lake, at the head of what was so appropriately called Emigration Canon. From that eyrie, 8,000 feet above tide water, the weary, starved, and ragged victim of Mormon proselyting first saw Zion, the object and end of his long wanderings, the holy and happy valley of the saints, and there the pilgrims, like the hajji of Mecca and Jerusalem, used to give way to the emotion so long buried under the dust and dangers of their journey over the plains, and break out into sobs and laughter, shouts of joy and hysterical tears. The women and children danced, the men chanted and sang psalms, and poor nervous creatures, broken down with fatigue, and distracted by hope deferred, gave vent to their joy and relief in contortions and demonstrations that were demoniacal.

It was said by the crafty saints that these hysterical displays were caused by religious fervor, but it was more the result of contrast between what had been endured behind and the sublime spectacle that lay before the mountains. All who have seen this valley in the verdure of spring—a lovely panorama of green and gold, azure and silver, with its background the rugged brows and black flanks of the Wahsatch Mountains, and its foreground a garden that looks in summer as if it were fresh from the hand of God—agree that there are few scenes in the world its equal for quiet picturesqueness and restful beauty. The atmosphere is so pure and so clear that distance is deceptive, and vision is bounded only by the bold, jagged outlines of the mountains in silhouette against the sky. The irrigation ditches for twenty or twenty-five miles up and down the valley are like silver threads in a brocade of green and gold, and far in the distance lies like a sheet of burnished silver that mystery of water, the Dead Sea.

The faithful saints truly believe, and none but the most arrant skeptic dare doubt, that in 1842, while they were slaves among the flesh-pots of Egypt, that the Creator of the world spread out this picture before Joseph Smith in a vision, as he showed the promised land to Moses from the top of Mount Pisgah 6,000 years before, and told him that he and his people should have this land to dwell in; that their children, and their children's children should abide here, and it should be theirs to possess and enjoy until the end of the world. Orson Pratt and Snow, the apostles who went out as pioneers to hunt "this oasis in the desert," as it was then called, were able, so they claim, when they reached Emigration Canon, to recognize in this landscape the promised land that had been pictured to them by the prophet many years before.

It is also believed that the spirit of the martyred prophet appeared to his successor, Brigham Young, and pointed out to him the proper location for the new temple, which was begun in 1853, and is still unfinished, although several million dollars have been expended. The glory will depart from the temple of Solomon when this structure is finished. It was designed by an Anglo-Mormon architect in 1852, and the architectural idea came by inspiration like all the rest of the faith. It will be a huge and complicated pile, a syncretism of Greek and Roman, Moorish and gothic, antique and modern. Each tile and timber, each stroke of the chisel is symbolical of something, but it simply bedazzles and bewilders the neophyte to hear the significance of its features described.

www.ingramcontent.com/pod-product-compliance
Lightning Source LLC
Chambersburg PA
CBHW020143170426
43199CB00010B/869